Population and nutrition

Ever since Malthus the insufficient supply of food resources has been considered the main constraint upon population growth and the main cause of the high rates of mortality prevailing in pre-industrial societies. In *Population and Nutrition* one of the world's leading demographers examines the mechanisms of biological, social and cultural nature linking subsistence, mortality and population and determining short- and long-term cycles in the latter. Professor Livi-Bacci examines the evidence from the Black Death to the onset of industrialisation, interpreting quantitative information on calorific budgets and food supply, prices and wages, changes in body height and epidemiological history, and contrasting demographic behaviour among the rich and poor. The picture that emerges casts doubt upon the existence of any long-term interrelationship between subsistence or nutritional levels and mortality, showing that the level of the latter was determined more by the epidemiological cycles than by the nutritional level of the population. The permanent potential conflict between food supply and population growth was also mediated by the biological adaptability of the human species to nutritional stress. In the short term the synergy between famine and epidemic infections in determining recurrent mortality crises is evident, but their impact starts declining in frequency and intensity in the eighteenth century.

Population and Nutrition provides a cogent introduction to many of the principal areas of demographic and historical debate, of interest to students and specialists in social history, historical geography, human biology and environmental science.

D1127215

Cambridge Studies in Population, Economy and
Society in Past Time 14

Series Editors:

PETER LASLETT, ROGER SCHOFIELD and E. A. WRIGLEY

ESRC Cambridge Group for the History of Population and Social Structure

and DANIEL SCOTT SMITH

University of Illinois at Chicago

Recent work in social, economic and demographic history has revealed much
that was previously obscure about societal stability and change in the past. It
has also suggested that crossing the conventional boundaries between these
branches of history can be very rewarding.

This series will exemplify the value of interdisciplinary work of this kind,
and will include books on topics such as family, kinship and neighbourhood;
welfare provision and social control; work and leisure; migration; urban
growth; and legal structures and procedures, as well as more familiar matters. It will demonstrate that, for example, anthropology and economics have
become as close intellectual neighbours to history as have political philo-
sophy or biography.

For a full list of titles in the series, please see end of book

Population and nutrition

An essay on European demographic history

MASSIMO LIVI-BACCI

TRANSLATED BY TANIA CROFT-MURRAY
WITH THE ASSISTANCE OF CARL IPSEN

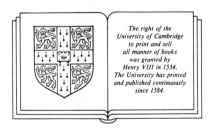

The right of the
University of Cambridge
to print and sell
all manner of books
was granted by
Henry VIII in 1534.
The University has printed
and published continuously
since 1584.

CAMBRIDGE UNIVERSITY PRESS

Cambridge
New York   Port Chester
Melbourne   Sydney

Published by the Press Syndicate of the University of Cambridge
The Pitt Building, Trumpington Street, Cambridge CB2 1RQ
40 West 20th Street, New York, NY 10011, USA
10 Stamford Road, Oakleigh, Melbourne 3166, Australia

Originally published in Italian as
Popolazione e Alimentazione: Saggio sulla storia demografica Europea
by Società editrice il Mulino, Bologna 1987
and © Società editrice il Mulino, Bologna 1987: 2nd edn 1989
First published in English by Cambridge University Press 1990 as
Population and nutrition: an essay on European demographic history

English translation © Cambridge University Press 1991

Printed in Great Britain by the Bath Press, Avon

British Library cataloguing in publication data
Livi-Bacci, Massimo
Population and nutrition: an essay on European
demographic history. – (Cambridge studies in population,
economy and society in past time; 14).
1.   Europe. Population. Growth. Nutritional factors, history
I.   Title II. Popolazione e alimentazione. *English*
304.62094

Library of Congress cataloguing in publication data
Livi-Bacci, Massimo.
Population and nutrition: an essay on European demographic history/
Massimo Livi-Bacci: translated by Tania Croft-Murray.
p.   cm. – (Cambridge studies in population, economy and society in past
time: 14)
Translation
Includes bibliographical references
ISBN 0 521 36325X. – ISBN 0 521 36871 5 (paperback)
1. Europe – Population – History. 2. Nutrition – Europe – History.
. Food supply – Europe – History. I. Title. II. Series.
HB3581.L58 1990   89-13895
04.6'094 – dc20   CIP

ISBN 0 521 36325 x hardback
ISBN 0 521 36871 5 paperback

Contents

v

vi

Figures

vii

Tables

ix

Preface

Before the cycle of plagues broke out in the fourteenth century, the population of Europe fell short of the 100 million mark; four centuries later, at the start of the Industrial Revolution, it was close on 150 million and had topped 300 million by the end of the nineteenth century. The quantitative history of Europe is beset by catastrophes, slow progress and periods of unstable stagnation and its aspect would undoubtedly have been quite different had its demographic growth been faster, or slower, than it actually was.

Here we have the outline of a fascinating topic for investigation: what made Europe develop in this manner rather than another? What were the forces which determined its demographic growth? Obviously, the long-term development of a population is closely linked to that of the material resources available to it, but this observation fails to satisfy our curiosity for three basic reasons. The first is that demographic development and the development of resources are not independent phenomena; their various movements interact, reinforcing or attenuating one another in ways as varied as they are numerous. The second reason is that the correlation between the two phenomena is only approximate; were it perfect there would not be some societies that, given the same level of demographic expansion, grew poor while others grew rich, nor would there be populations that, given the same degree of economic expansion, grew a great deal while others grew only a little. The third reason is that while the demographic phenomena which determine the response or the adaptation of a population to the development of resources are fairly well understood in terms of their mechanical function (we are able to analyse mortality, fertility and mobility provided we have sufficient data), the same cannot be said for their causal origins.

xi

Demographic development can be seen as resulting from the opposing action of forces of constraint and forces of choice. The forces of constraint are tied to environmental limitations, the hostility of the climate, the poverty of the food supply and to epidemic attacks. Mankind can control these only to some extent and over long periods of time, usually periods which exceed the average human lifespan. The forces of choice which are demographically relevant are those which affect the processes of family formation, levels of fertility and the occupation of new territory. These forces of choice enable individuals to adapt themselves and react to the forces of constraint. They ensure the flexibility of demographic aggregates essential for survival. The traditional demographic regime was characterised by strong forces of constraint. As such, the space allowed to demographic expansion in the long term was fairly limited, allowing at best a rate of growth of a few units per thousand population per year. Nonetheless, mathematics of growth are such that even a minute difference in the pattern of increase will, over a long time-span, give rise to strong differentials in population.

The availability of food and its related nutritional models have in general been viewed as the primary factors of demographic constraint in the traditional regime. The theory which sees in the availability of nourishment the principal force affecting the pace of demographic change has always enjoyed considerable favour. It is a theory that appeals strongly to common sense: the growth cycles of plants and animals show that plenitude or poverty of resources (land or food) mean expansion or contraction of the species. For man, as for animals, malnutrition is inextricably linked to physical decline and disease, just as an abundance and variety of food is thought to be the basis of strength and good health. The nutrition factor then becomes, alone or in conjunction with others, the dominant explanatory factor of the great European cycles. It helps to explain both the destructive violence of the plague cycles, exacerbated by the nutritional problems of populations which had outgrown their available resources, and the demographic acceleration of the eighteenth century fuelled by greater agricultural productivity and the introduction of new crops.

This study confronts the issue of the interdependence of food, survival and population. The 'nutritional hypothesis' will be tested as we look for proofs and pointers in the rich fields of biology and epidemiology, not to mention those of economic and social history. The results are complex. In the short term, the negative effects of poverty and famine (coinciding with epidemic outbreaks) on population are well established, even though the greatest mortality crises have generally been brought about by epidemics not linked to nutritional factors. In the long term, however, there appears to be no real relation between nutrition and demographic development. There are three reasons for this non-verification of the nutritional hypothesis. The first is contingent upon the lack of empirical knowledge about the demographic facts on the one hand, and the history of nutrition on the other. Demographic patterns in the eighteenth and nineteenth centuries are fairly well defined, but become increasingly less so the further we go back in time. The history of nutrition for most of the period under consideration is based on circumstantial evidence, and the significance of the main indicators – prices, wages, food budgets, height – is uncertain and debatable. The second reason, like the third, questions the very substance of the nutritional hypothesis. The available indicators, uncertain as they may be, lead to the conclusion that, at least in normal periods, food supplies were adequate and ensured a decent level of survival, and that virtually no correlation existed between the type or level of nutrition and mortality rates. This is demonstrated by comparing social classes and groups, historical periods, or communities enjoying substantially different levels of nutrition. Besides, there was no correlation between the virulence of cyclical epidemics, often exogenous in origin to the system (such as the plague or smallpox) and levels of nutrition. The third reason, finally, is largely biological or socio-biological in nature. Populations possess a remarkable degree of adaptability to nutritional stress, both in the short and medium term – a fact all too often underestimated – which mitigates (though certainly does not do away with) the conflict between nutritional deprivation and human survival.

There are those who have suggested to me, and I believe with some justification, that the attempt to subdivide the phenomenon of underdevelopment – caused by poverty, poor hygiene, ignorance, malnutrition and sickness – is antihistorical and in some sense naive. They attribute this not only to the scarcity of factual information that I have mentioned above, but also to the impossibility of unravelling the tangle of causes that have led historically to high mortality rates and slow demographic growth. Perhaps such an attempt is antihistorical, but it is certainly not 'antidemographic', demography being a discipline that attempts, where possible, to disentangle complex phenomena like those which contributed to the high mortality rates of the past. Moreover, it is interesting to emphasise that the lively debate currently taking place on the factors which determine the low survival rate in less developed countries has important political and practical implications. Indeed, how do we reduce the incidence of infant and child mortality? Is it better to improve nutrition, to alter the environment, or to provide medical or hygiene aid? Clearly, not everything can be done at once. What is important is to tackle the variables that have the most impact on this global phenomenon.

  This essay was inspired by a course held for Ph.D. students at the University of Berkeley, California, in 1985 and by another for doctoral students in Demography in Florence in 1986. Debates and discussions with the students encouraged me to enter into a deeper study of this subject and to put together a book out of my sketchy ideas. I have also conducted a series of seminars on this subject at various universities: Padua, Milan, Pisa, Florence and Siena; in Paris at the Institut d'Etudes Politiques; in Madrid at the Fundación Ortega y Gasset; and finally in the United States at Stanford and Princeton Universities. The complexity of the subject – large areas of which lie outside my domain – has made it necessary for me to seek the help and advice of friends and colleagues much more than I am used to doing when confronted with challenging issues that, however, remain within the safe area of my discipline. My deepest gratitude to all involved.

1

Demographic growth in Europe

Quantitative growth

During the first half of the eighteenth century, before the Industrial Revolution hit full stride and the Scientific Revolution yielded up the results of its manifold inventions in the technical and medical fields, the population of Western Europe amounted to about 100 million, a large population perhaps three times that estimated to have occupied the same territory in the time of Augustus. It was the culmination of almost two millennia of demographic vicissitudes and the starting point for a new leap forward that (in less than two centuries) would see population triple once again.

The tripling of the population between the beginning of the common era and the eighteenth century was not a gradual process but the result of successive waves of crisis and expansion: crisis in the late Imperial and Justinian age marked by barbaric invasions and the plague; expansion in the twelfth and thirteenth centuries; followed by another devastating crisis in the mid-fourteenth century brought on by the repeated visitations of the Black Death; strong recovery from mid-fifteenth to the end of the sixteenth century; followed by crisis, or stagnation, until the beginning of the eighteenth century, at which point the forces of modern expansion began to gather momentum.[1]

The pattern of European population growth is compared to that of the world in Figure 1 and Table 1. The figures in this table and the curve of the graph should be taken only as a rough guide to the past and not as an accurate measure. Our knowledge of the past is still far from satisfactory and, for long historical periods and vast continents, it is destined to remain so. Indeed, the sources of the data given in the graph by and large decrease in accuracy the further back one goes in time. The earliest sources must be regarded as little more than qualitative indicators (historical documents, numbers of settlements, limits

1

Table 1 *World population by area, 1200–1900*

Year	Inhabitants (millions)				% Distribution			
	Europe	Asia	Other	World	Europe	Asia	Other	World
1200	71	257	89	417	17.0	61.6	21.3	100
1340	90	238	114	442	20.4	53.8	25.8	100
1400	65	201	109	375	17.3	53.6	29.1	100
1500	84	245	132	461	18.2	53.1	28.6	100
1600	111	338	129	578	19.2	58.5	22.3	100
1700	125	433	122	680	18.4	63.7	17.9	100
1750	146	500	125	771	18.9	64.9	16.2	100
1800	195	631	128	954	20.4	66.1	13.4	100
1850	288	790	163	1241	23.2	63.7	13.1	100
1900	422	903	309	1634	25.8	55.3	18.9	100

Source: J. N. Biraben, 'Essai sur l'évolution du nombre des hommes', in *Population*, 34 (1979), no. 1, pp. 13–25.

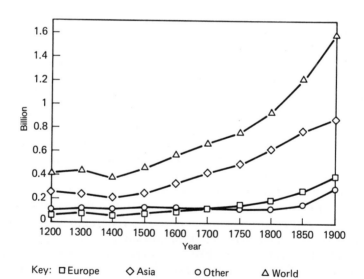

Key: □ Europe   ◇ Asia   ○ Other   △ World

Figure 1 World population by continent, 1200–1900
Source: J. M. Biraben, 'Essai sur l'évolution du nombre des hommes', *Population*, 34 (1979), no. 1, pp. 13–25.

of cultured land), indicators that are turned into figures with difficulty, however cleverly we may try to manipulate them. Nonetheless, the pattern of alternating crisis, stagnation and growth is broadly speaking that given in Figure 1.

If we limit our observations to Europe and its main regions, we are able to make some other general observations. The first is that demographic growth, when calculated in terms of centuries rather than short periods marked by the tremendous fluctuations precipitated by war and want, epidemics and other catastrophes, was apparently rather slow. During the relatively long period from 1200 to 1700 the average annual rate of growth was barely 1.3 per thousand. Assuming a death-rate of the order of 35 per thousand, the birth-rate would have been about 4 per cent higher (36.3 per thousand). However, the growth rate varied considerably from century to century. The thirteenth, fifteenth and sixteenth centuries enjoyed substantial increases (around 3 per thousand), whereas the fourteenth century was marked by a severe decline (-3 per thousand) and the seventeenth by stagnation. It seems, then, that throughout this period Europe was able, in the absence of serious crisis, to maintain an annual rate of increase of 3 per thousand. This rate may seem small to us, accustomed as we are to the accelerated growth rates of the developing countries of the present century, easily ten times greater. Such high rates of growth, however, could not have been sustained for protracted periods, given the available fixed (spatial) and variable responses. Over the five centuries preceding the seventeenth, even though growth in two of these was nil or negative, the population of Europe did almost double. With the advent of the eighteenth, and especially the nineteenth, centuries the traditional barriers to population growth were removed; growth exceeded 4 per thousand per annum in the former, and 7 per thousand in the latter, and the population tripled. Particular attention has been focussed on this later period, rightly considered exceptional for the demographic transformation it witnessed: reduction in fertility and mortality, and changes in the life cycle of the individual and the family. What is even more astonishing, however, is the fact that, in spite of the forces of constraint which hindered its growth, the population doubled over those five centuries between 1200 and 1700.

Another aspect of the demographic growth of Europe which merits consideration is the uniformity and variation in the growth patterns of the various sub-populations. Figure 2 shows the relative force of population increase for six large national areas from 1200 to 1850, expressed as a percentage of European average growth. In Figure 2, a

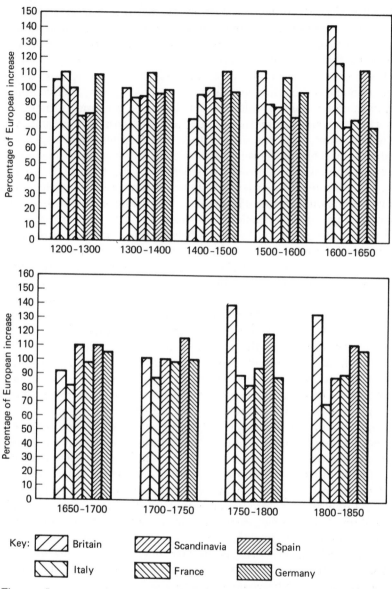

Figure 2 Increases of six populations as a percentage of European growth
Source: Data processed by V. Perez Moreda and D. S. Reher, 'Demographic
Mechanisms and Long-Term Swings in Populations in Europe, 1200–1850',
International Population Conference (Florence, 1985), vol. 4 of the proceedings,
pp. 313–29.

growth index of 100 (like that of France between 1650 and 1700) is equivalent to that of the whole continent during the same period; an index over or under 100 indicates that the growth rate was higher or lower than the European rate, during the same time-span. The diagram shows that, except for the periods 1600–50 and after 1750, the growth rates of the sub-populations were relatively uniform. This indicates that, at least until the middle of the eighteenth century, the same factors affected different demographic structures in similar ways, resulting on the whole in geographically homogeneous growth. (Any dissimilarities over the years 1600–50 can probably be attributed to staggered cycles and to the effects of the Thirty Years War.) In the earlier period, at least, it may be that this homogeneity is attributable to biased 'estimates' of population size made in the different areas, so I shall not dwell further on them.

More recently, that is after 1600, population estimates become undoubtedly more reliable. They enable us to set up Table 2, showing the populations of England, France, Holland, Germany, Spain and Italy in 1600 (before the outbreak of the last plague cycle and the Thirty Years War), in 1750 and in 1850. From 1600 to 1850, but especially in the years 1600–1750, five of the populations under consideration reveal very uniform behaviour, the one outstanding exception being England. Over these two and a half centuries the population of England quadrupled, against a bare doubling in other countries.[2]

Table 2 also shows that at the end of the demographic *ancien régime* (a telling if somewhat imprecise definition) around 1750, the populations of Europe had attained comparable densities of about fifty inhabitants per square kilometre, the one exception being Spain, historically sparsely populated. Estimated values refer to present day boundaries. For Germany, to the German Federal Republic and German Democratic Republic; for Spain, only to the mainland. For France, Italy and Spain the estimated data are based on that given by the quoted authors and are our own. It would of course be dangerous to assume that density is an indicator of 'demographic pressure' or of the relationship between population and resources. Nevertheless, this similarity between populations could be something more than simple coincidence.

The space for demographic growth

I have already shown that during the late Middle Ages and early modern period in Europe, the average rate of growth was rather low, around 1.3 per thousand per annum and that, for sufficiently long

Table 2 *The development of six European populations, 1600–1850*

Country	Population (millions)			Indices			Density pop/kil²	Distribution %		
	1600	1750	1850	1750 (1600=100)	1850 (1750=100)	1850 (1600=100)	1750	1600	1750	1850
England	4.1	5.7	16.5	139	289	402	47	7	8	14
Holland	1.5	1.9	3.1	127	163	207	63	3	3	2
Germany	12.0	15.0	27.0	125	180	225	42	22	21	22
France	19.0	25.0	35.8	132	143	188	46	34	34	29
Italy	12.0	15.7	24.8	131	158	207	52	22	22	20
Spain	6.8	8.4	14.5	124	173	213	17	12	12	12
Total	55.4	71.7	121.7	129	170	220		100	100	100

Sources: Data inferred or based on the following works: England: E. A. Wrigley and R. Schofield, *The Population History of England 1541–1871* (London, 1981), pp. 532–4; Holland: B. H. Slicher Van Bath, 'Historical Demography and the Social and Economic Development of the Netherlands', in *Daedalus*, Spring 1968, p. 609; Germany: C. McEvedy and R. Jones, *Atlas of World Population History* (London, 1978), pp. 67–70; France: J. Dupâquier, *La population française au XVIIe et XVIII siècles* (Paris, 1979), pp. 9 and 11; Italy: C. M. Cipolla, 'Four Centuries of Italian Demographic Development', in D. V. Glass and D. E. C. Eversley (eds.), *Population in History* (London, 1965). p. 571; Spain: J. Nadal, *La Población Española* (Barcelona, 1984). p. 17.

periods and sufficiently large populations, it seldom exceeded 3 per thousand. For all their quantitative precision, these figures tell us nothing about the factors which govern growth; nor is it particularly useful to state that a growth rate of 1 per thousand, given a death-rate of 35 per thousand, means that the birth-rate exceeded the latter by 1 point, assuming no migratory exchanges. It is therefore more useful to examine the rhythm of growth in the light of other measures of human mortality and fertility, measures much closer to intuitive concepts of life and death.

Let us suppose we are dealing with populations locked into a fixed demographic regime. Demographers call this state of affairs 'stability', understanding by this expression fixed levels of mortality and fertility. Historically, stability occurs only in exceptional cases, as catastrophes and gradual changes in behavioural patterns affect mortality and fertility levels. However, if we do not impose overly restrictive conditions, and content ourselves with an approximation to stability – that is, a relatively fixed situation such as might endure over a long historical period and during which the various (demographic) oscillations compensate one another – then our argument can be applied to many historical populations. Clearly, in order to maintain a population at a constant level (zero growth rate), it is necessary for successive generations of parents and children to be in numerical equilibrium. For this to occur it is necessary, on average, for every boy or girl who comes into this world to produce during the course of his or her life a boy or a girl. This idea is better understood if we look at a hypothetical group of one thousand new-born baby girls. Supposing that, during the course of their lives, these girls give birth to a total of another one thousand girls, then the generations are in perfect equilibrium (at replacement level). If this behaviour is repeated over generations, the population will have a growth rate equal to zero. If, on the other hand, the daughters exceed one thousand, or fall short of it, the result will be a tendency for population increase or decrease. Increase, stagnation, or reduction depend on the intensity of procreation by each couple and the intensity of mortality. The ratio of daughters to the generation of the mothers is a measure of the fertility of the population, easily translatable as a rate of increase. It can be expressed as either of two well-known demographic measures: the gross reproduction rate, GRR (where GRR denotes theoretical number of daughters born to each woman during her reproductive life-span, assuming no deaths); and the measure of survival, life expectancy at birth, e_o.[3]

We shall now attempt to identify the 'space' in which the demographic growth of past populations took place as a function of these two easily understood concepts: the average number of children born per woman in the absence of mortality, GRR, and length of life expressed as life expectancy at birth, e_o. The term 'space' describes the ability of every population to follow a particular path of demographic growth as a function of various combinations of GRR and e_o; this concept implies the existence of diversified growth 'strategies'. The space within which these strategies may occur is defined by the biological and social characteristics of each species, characteristics which set limits on life-span or on the number of children who may be born. For example, in biology we speak of two opposing strategic models among animal species, corresponding to two alternative patterns of selection: r and K.[4] Strategy type r pertains to very small organisms with a short life-span, short intervals between generations and a high reproductive potential. This strategy is particularly suitable in unstable and sparsely populated environments, given that the capacity of the species to proliferate is very high and their numbers are subject to violent cycles of growth and diminution. Micro-organisms, insects, some fish and small mammals fall into this category. The opposite strategy, type K, is suited to large animals with long life-spans, long generation intervals and high parental investment for a relatively small number of offspring. K strategy is suited to stable environments in which individuals compete for available resources and experience lower fluctuations in their numbers. It is typical of men and of the larger mammals. It is obviously hazardous to apply the concepts of animal biology to human behaviour. Nevertheless, it is certainly true that human populations, in their efforts to balance the forces of choice and constraint, do not all behave in the same fashion, and it is interesting to note within which limits, or spaces, these variations occur.

Figure 3 shows a series of curves which I shall call isogrowth curves. Each curve corresponds to those combinations of life expectancy (the abscissa, e_o) and number of daughters per mother (the ordinate, GRR) which result in a certain growth rate.[5] Life expectancies lower than fifteen or higher than forty-five are not given; in the case of the former because they are not compatible with the survival of the species; in the case of the latter because they were never realised in pre-modern societies. By the same token, reproduction rates of over five (implying an average of ten children per woman, quite possible in individual cases but not realisable by a large population), or of less than two (with rare exceptions communities in the past did not practise birth control), are not considered. The space

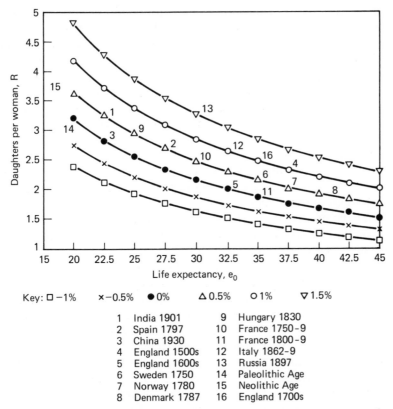

Key: □ −1%   × −0.5%   ● 0%   △ 0.5%   ○ 1%   ▽ 1.5%

1	India 1901	9	Hungary 1830
2	Spain 1797	10	France 1750-9
3	China 1930	11	France 1800-9
4	England 1500s	12	Italy 1862-9
5	England 1600s	13	Russia 1897
6	Sweden 1750	14	Paleolithic Age
7	Norway 1780	15	Neolithic Age
8	Denmark 1787	16	England 1700s

Figure 3 The relationship between fertility, R, life expectancy, e_o, and growth, r

described in Figure 3 also contains some examples of actual 'historical' populations. These examples differ somewhat in their validity, being drawn in some cases from direct and reliable observations, and estimated in others from indirect, scant and fragmentary information. Others are pure conjecture.

The populations of Figure 3 are all within the band ranging from increases of 1.5 per cent to decreases of 0.5 per cent. But the majority of these lie in the band 0−0.5, which accords with our observations for European populations. Yet within this narrow band, location of the various populations varies considerably, owing to sharply differing combinations of fertility and mortality. Denmark at the end of the eighteenth century and India at the beginning of this one had similar rates of growth, but reached with widening diverging locations in the strategic space: the first with a high life expectancy, around forty years of age, and low fertility; the second with low life expectancy, around twenty-five years, but high reproductive patterns. Palaeolithic populations, which practised hunting and gathering, and neolithic ones, which practised settled cultivation, occupied different locations though they experienced very similar rates of growth. According to one fairly widely held opinion, mortality in the first case was probably lower because of a lower density of population, unfavourable to the occurrence and spreading of contagious disease; whilst fertility was moderate because of the high level of mobility, incompatible with a high burden of children per woman. In the populations of the neolithic, the same rate of growth was obtained because of high mortality and high reproduction as a result of higher density and lower mobility.

While Figure 3 may be a good representation of the strategic space of growth, it is nonetheless a very simplified one. I shall not discuss mortality, because it can be considered in the first analysis as being determined by external constraints only slightly susceptible to change by human action. This, again, is only true in part because, as we shall see below, culturally determined behaviour patterns can have a marked effect on survival even before the age of great medical and sanitary progress. As far as fertility is concerned, it can be broken down into many other factors, some chiefly biological in character (the level of so-called natural fertility, in turn affected by sanitary conditions, nutritional levels, length of nursing periods, frequency of sexual intercourse and so forth), others mainly social and cultural (access to reproduction, usually determined by marriage and hence by age at marriage, proportion remaining single, frequency of second marriage and so forth). If we look at the history of human populations as a difficult equilibrium between the forces of constraint and those of choice, we can say that the former have had a greater influence on mortality and the latter on fertility.

In this essay, while not overlooking the effect that variations in fertility (GRR) have had on the use of strategic space, I shall concentrate primarily on the effect of variations in mortality and therefore on the factors of constraint which have determined its level throughout history. Of the various factors of constraint I shall consider in particular that of nutrition.

Food resources and population

Even before Malthus, Adam Smith defined the close link existing between demographic development and availability of resources in a sentence which is as famous as it is obvious: 'every species of animal naturally multiplies in proportion to the means of their subsistence, and no species can ever multiply beyond it'.[6] There is no doubt that by means of subsistence Smith meant above all basic material necessities, and especially food. A few decades later Malthus, in his *Essay*, was to repeat that 'food is necessary to the existence of man' and that 'the power of population is indefinitely greater than the power in the earth to produce subsistence for man'. Where again means of subsistence is above all food, its lack or scarcity promotes 'misery' and vice and so leads to a high incidence of infant mortality and epidemic disease. Of course human toil, poor clothing and inadequate housing all contributed to misery, yet without a doubt its most salient cause was the lack or scarcity of food. This clear link was stated often, in various forms and circumstances, in different editions of the *Essay*. Nor does Ricardo have any doubts in this matter twenty years later: 'In those countries where the labouring classes have the fewest wants, and are contented with the cheapest food, the people are exposed to the greatest vicissitudes and miseries.' And further on he states that it is the low price of food in America, and its high price in Europe, that accelerates demographic growth in the first case and slows it down in the second.[8]

The opinion of the classical economists reflected a self-evident truth. In rural societies where farming was the chief source of wealth, people worked to clothe and house themselves, but above all to fulfil the basic need of feeding themselves, and the availability of food was the limiting factor *par excellence*. Even in cities, where only a small proportion of the population lived, shop-assistants and shopkeepers, workmen and craftsmen spent almost their whole income on food. Even as late as the mid-nineteenth century, societies in the cultural and scientific vanguard, like France and Germany, had not completely solved the food problems of the whole population. Whereas, during periods relatively free of the vagaries of climate and the catastrophes of war, food levels proved adequate, in years of shortage and famine caused by the failure of one or more harvests, food consumption for most people must have been severely reduced.

Malthus outlined a model in which populations and resources were inexorably linked. The ability of a population to multiply causes the relationship between resources and inhabitants to deteriorate until that dangerous point is reached at which the repressive checks of famine, disease and war reduce the size of the population and restore the uneasy equilibrium with resources. However, if the capacity of the population to expand is not otherwise checked a new negative cycle will eventually be established. Such a check does exist; it is the preventive and virtuous check of marital restraint, the practice of delaying or avoiding marriage and so reducing the growth of that population which wisely follows Malthus' advice. It is the conflict between positive and preventive checks, between thoughtless and virtuous behaviour, between being a victim of constraint or need, or having freedom to choose, which determines the fate of a population.[9]

Out of the Malthusian model – continually restated and updated to the present day but retraceable in its foundations to the essential logic of its first formulation – a number of fixed points emerge:

1 Resources are, above all, food resources. Their scarcity results in an increase in mortality and thus in a slowing or reversing of population

2 Increases in production and productivity as a consequence of technical progress provide only temporary relief. Inevitably the beneficial effect is reabsorbed by demographic growth

3 An awareness of the vicious circle of positive checks on demographic expansion may induce a population to forestall excessive growth by lowering nuptiality

In more recent formulations, nuptiality is integrated into the Malthusian cycle described in the first point. Figure 4 shows the relationship between preventive checks, positive checks and population cycles (one in a phase of growth and the other in a phase of decline). For each phase the diagram shows two paths, according to whether the preventive check on marriage is operating (path 1) or not (path 2). If it is operating, then an increase in population will be accompanied by a shortage of food and an increase in prices. Work will be less well paid as a consequence of the growing supply of workers, and real wages will drop. The drop in real wages and the ensuing deterioration in living conditions will give rise to a significant reduction in nuptiality and a weak increase in mortality. In this case, demographic decline occurs partly through a rise in mortality and partly through a reduction in the marriage- and birth-rates. If, on the other hand, the preventive check is not operating (path 2), then a drop in real wages, having little effect on the nuptiality, will result primarily in higher mortality. However, a sharp rise in mortality weakly stimulates nuptiality by creating, by way of inheritance, opportunities for the creation of households (opening of 'niches'). This in turn neutralises the negative effect of the reduction of real wages. In this case a reduction in population is solely a consequence of an increase in mortality.

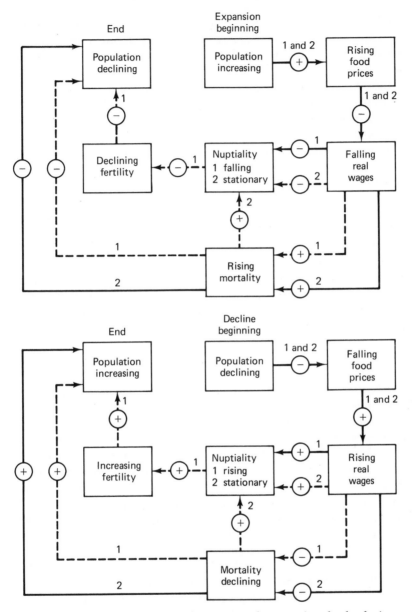

Figure 4 The Malthusian system of positive and preventive checks during a
period of demographic expansion and one of decline
Note: The direction of the arrows indicates the assumed direction of
causality; + or − indicates the positive or negative effect on the succeeding
phenomenon. A dotted line indicates a more tenuous link than a continuous
line. Route 1 indicates strong birth-rate and Route 2 a weaker one.

When a population grows, food becomes scarcer and its price goes up, work is less well paid as a result of its increased supply, and real wages go down. Living conditions, being harder, lead to an increase in mortality and at the same time to a reduction in fertility as a result of the smaller number of marriages. The negative demographic cycle, brought about by the scarcity of resources, causes the population to diminish (as after the cycle of plagues in the fourteenth century or after the Thirty Years War). A smaller population means greater resources for each inhabitant and lower food prices, not to mention better compensation of labour due to a reduced supply of workers. However, improved living conditions for the population bear within them the germ of their negation. Indeed, marriages will become more frequent and the population will grow until it encounters the inevitable negative cycle.

Nutrition has therefore two effects on demographic growth, a direct one and an indirect one. Nutritional fluctuations lead to synchronous fluctuations in mortality. This is the direct effect. These fluctuations also produce fluctuations in the access to marriage, which in its turn affects fertility and hence the rate of growth. This is the indirect effect.

Demographic trends: theories and interpretations

The limited information we have about growth in European populations raises a series of questions, questions which scholars have attempted to answer using a variety of approaches. In addressing some of these problems, I shall try to illustrate the kinds of answers that have been offered. The main queries are these: what caused the alternation of phases of expansion, stagnation and decline? Why in some periods should there be differential growth between different populations? What caused the onset of rapid growth in the eighteenth century? Were the great epidemics the principal factor affecting demographic growth and were their cycles attributable to factors exogenous or endogenous to society? What effect did nutrition have on demographic growth? Did nuptiality obey rigid models or actually respond and shape itself according to the needs of the various historical periods? An exhaustive account of the arguments for and against the various interpretations would take me too far off my intended course; but a brief survey of some of them, with the aid of concrete examples, may help to better define my route. I shall limit myself to a few cases dealing with large populations and long periods of time.

The English case has been widely discussed thanks to the recent reconstruction by Wrigley and Schofield of English population history from the sixteenth to the late nineteenth centuries.[10] This example conforms well to the Malthusian model: in the long term, phases of demographic growth were characterised by rising prices and declining real wages; while phases of demographic decline or stagnation were characterised by falling prices, rising real wages, and therefore improved living standards. In the English case, however, the demographic component determining changes in the rate of population growth is not mortality – which appears not to be correlated with phases of economic prosperity or crisis – but rather nuptiality and therefore fertility. When the standard of living deteriorates – because as the population increases so do prices while real wages decline – nuptiality declines and so allows for an adjustment between the economy and population. When population stagnates, prices slacken, real wages rise, and nuptiality – and so also fertility – increases initiating growth and with it a new cycle. In England, the restraint of the population allowed nuptiality to regulate demographic expansion and thus prevented the repressive check of high mortality from coming into operation. There prevailed, therefore, a system of 'low demographic pressure', as defined by Wrigley and Schofield: nuptiality, a 'providential thermostat' we might say, prevented demographic pressure from building up excessively and setting in motion repressive mechanisms.

In contrast to the English example there is that of France, at least during the seventeenth and eighteenth centuries, which might be considered one of high demographic pressure. Here it was primarily mortality that checked demographic growth, keeping the system in a state of unhappy equilibrium. This classic interpretation, expressed most completely by Pierre Goubert,[11] is supported by the fact that, by contrast with England, the intensity and frequency of demographic crises caused by subsistence crises are much higher, particularly up until the second half of the eighteenth century. J. Dupâquier has in part contested Goubert's interpretations, seeing the explanation for French demographic trends not so much in terms of demographic crises as in the inherent rigidity of the economic system, at least as far as the north is concerned.[12] The rules of matrimony were rigid and unalterable, and were based on three tenets: child-bearing outside wedlock was not tolerated (a rule, moreover, upheld in most of Europe); young married couples did not cohabitate with their parents (a rule applying in the North and the Bassin Parisien, but not in other parts of France where the principle of the stem family prevailed); no marriage could take place unless a 'niche' was available. In French society, almost exclusively rural, it was virtually impossible to acquire land. It belonged to the Church and aristocracy who rented it out, and at best, peasants were owners of small indivisible holdings. Available land was scarce. For all these reasons, setting up a new household was practically impossible unless an existing 'niche' became vacant. The system was jammed by the impossibility of increasing the number of dwellings or niches. Such an unbending marriage system lacked the responsiveness to economic events characteristic of the English system. This increased demographic pressure, as reflected in the greater intensity and frequency of demographic crises associated with subsistence crises.

Somewhere between England and northern France lies the interesting case of Ireland. If estimates based on unreliable counts are anything to go by, Ireland experienced a demographic boom in the second half of the eighteenth century, despite extremely backward conditions. According to Connell,[13] the Irish population increased 250 per cent in the century preceding the Great Famine of 1845. Apparently neither repressive nor preventive checks curtailed growth. The introduction of the potato and its diffusion during the second half of the eighteenth century increased productivity, enabling smallholders and tenants to subdivide their land and create space for new households. As a result, population grew. The preventive checks did not operate and the rapid population increase paved the way for the disastrous famine crisis of the 1840s. Of still greater interest, the experience of this crisis left such a deep mark on the social fabric of Ireland as to cause fundamental changes in marital customs. Marriage tended to occur later, celibacy became common, and land was available to children only on the death of their parents. Before 1845, the system was one of high pressure and as such the creation of space for new households led to demographic expansion. But the system was doomed to collapse. The case is diametrically opposed to the English one, though the demographic increase is surprisingly similar, at least until the middle of the nineteenth century.

A clear-cut Malthusian model is offered in Le Roy Ladurie's classic study of the history of the people of Languedoc over many centuries.[14] He discovered alternating cycles of growth, stagnation and decline beginning with a period of medieval expansion saturating a system already fragile before the plague of 1348. (Other studies have found similar trends during the two centuries preceding the plague, whether in Italy, England, Germany or France.) Populations

expanded, occupying marginal lands and higher altitudes where productivity is low. The late thirteenth and first half of the fourteenth
centuries reveal evidence of repeated famines and a slackening of
demographic growth. Then the Black Death broke out and decimated
the population. The diminished population caused an aggregation of
households and land-ownership, which endured until demographic
recovery became sustained, gaining momentum in the sixteenth century. Land again became scarce, and fragmentation systematic.
Increasingly less productive land was brought into cultivation. The
country became poorer, demographic growth weaker, and at the turn
of the seventeenth century population declined. Although famine
and mortality crises were not as marked as in the north, poverty, high
mortality in normal years and low nuptiality produced a demographic
crisis. A more favourable equilibrium was established after the reign
of Louis XIV.

These alternating cycles of growth, stagnation and decline are
interpreted by Le Roy Ladurie in Malthusian terms. Population out-
grows its resources and eventually encounters repressive checks;
population decreases and a new cycle begins. Similar interpretations
have been given for other areas in southern Europe: Catalonia, Provence and various parts of Italy.[15]

There are, therefore, two mechanisms operating on the demographic history of the half millennium we are dealing with: the variations in mortality which, according to orthodox Malthusian opinion,
bear a direct relation to the abundance or scarcity of resources; and
the speed with which family households are formed (nuptiality), this
often depending on the availability of land and the possibility of
creating new dwellings. When land is available – either because a low
density of population makes it possible for new land to be cultivated,
or because large states are subdivided, or because greater productivity enables two families to survive where only one survived
before – then the nuptiality mechanism leads to population growth.
This probably explains the sharp population increase in the great
plains of eastern Europe (land availability); in Ireland (as productivity
grew, land could be subdivided); in thirteenth-century Europe (deforestation and drainage made more land available though with decreas-
ing yields); and in sixteenth-century Holland (land suitable for
cultivation was reclaimed from the sea).

One salient doubt remains concerning the causes behind variations
in mortality. As we have seen, Malthusian orthodoxy would link
these to the availability of sustenance even though, in Malthus'
homeland, variations occurring between the sixteenth and late

nineteenth centuries had little to do with cycles of prosperity and depression. It seems certain that they also depended on other factors which had little to do with the availability of sustenance, namely the intensity, frequency and length of epidemic cycles. In fact an 'epidemiological' explanation is quite plausible, given the synchronism of demographic cycles across different populations, and especially given the synchronism of the onset and cessation of the plagues. Scholars like Helleiner and Cipolla,[16] while not excluding other more complex explanations, seem to favour this one above the rest. Moreover, the epidemiological explanation makes the death-rate a factor 'exogenous' to society. In other words, it is not a lowering of the standard of living brought about by demographic increase that stimulates mortality (repressive checks) as in the Malthusian scheme and its adaptations; the epidemic cycle (particularly that of the plague) is independent of living conditions and is the consequence of a complex balance between pathogenic germs, their virulence and the human immune system, having little or nothing to do with standard of living.

Demographic cycles and nutritional revolutions

Let us now consider the means of subsistence, the production and consumption of food, and the nutritional state of the population. According to the Malthusian formula the availability of sustenance correlates directly with the action of the repressive check, that is mortality. In the opinion of many writers it was the improvement in agricultural production methods, and thus in nutritional standards, from the eighteenth century onwards that encouraged demographic growth, largely by reducing mortality. The hypothesis that there exists a direct link between nutrition and mortality, and to a lesser extent between nutrition and epidemic cycles, seems plausible. This belief is supported by two self-evident observations: the first is the obvious association between undernourishment and the risk of death; the second is the equally obvious coincidence of great famine and peaks of mortality. Yet recognition of these two relationships is not proof in itself of the existence of a direct correlation between demographic or mortality cycles and the fluctuating availability of sustenance. Firstly, we must ascertain the nutritional thresholds below which the risk of death increases, and whether these thresholds were regularly or only intermittently crossed in the period under consideration, and by what proportion of the population. Secondly, we must determine which mortality crises were associated with famines and whether or not these did actually account for the majority of deaths. We shall see that the answers to these two questions are by no means straightforward.

Let us return to the proponents of nutrition as the primary factor in the demographic cycle. The most prominent and authoritative voice is that of McKeown who, in a book and numerous essays, has forcefully presented his point of view to population historians.[17] We can condense this as follows: (a) The demographic expansion occurring in England and other parts of Europe from the eighteenth century onwards is attributable to the population's improved nutritional standards. In fact, neither the progress of medical practice and health care, nor improved private or public hygiene, nor for that matter any other factors, are capable of explaining the decline in mortality. Moreover, at least in England, expansion seems to be attributable to a decline in mortality and not to an increase in fertility. (b) Before the eighteenth century, the modest demographic increase across a period of centuries can be put down to poor nutrition and the limited production and availability of food, since improvement in the availability of food is an indispensable condition for a reduction in mortality and for long-term demographic expansion.

McKeown's hypothesis, like many apparently self-evident assertions, is open to criticism, although this is not our main concern here. It seems reasonable to note that demographic acceleration in the eighteenth century occurred in many areas of Europe where there was no nutritional improvement, and also where there was, if anything, a nutritional deterioration. In several countries, most conspicuously England, it was the variations in nuptiality and fertility, rather than in mortality, that determined demographic cycles. This applies especially to eighteenth-century growth. But reserving criticism for later, let us pass on to what is of interest to us at the conclusion of this introductory first chapter and discuss whether the nutritional revolution of the eighteenth century, studied by McKeown, and the two revolutions which preceded it, brought with them analogous revolutions in the life expectancy of the populations concerned, the history of which is shown schematically in Figure 5. The three revolutions which I shall consider are the neolithic, the late medieval and that of the eighteenth century.

The first of these revolutions was caused by a gradual transition from the system of hunting and gathering practised by nomadic populations to one of settled agriculture. Opinion is divided as to what effect this extraordinary revolution in the production and consumption of food had on the demography of the populations who

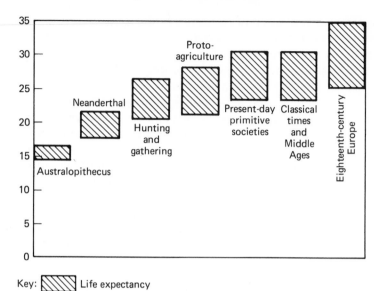

Figure 5 Life expectancy in some populations
Source: Adapted from K. H. Weiss, 'Demographic Models for
Anthropology', *American Antiquity*, 38 (1973), no. 2, part II, p. 49.

undertook it. Classical opinion, well expressed by Childe, affirms that
this revolution resulted in a net improvement in the nutritional
regime, providing a more stable and abundant food supply and one
obtained with less effort. As a result of the greater availability of
sustenance, and presumably of improved life expectancy, the population enjoyed more dynamic growth.[18] This theory has been systematically attacked in recent decades. In fact, hunters and gatherers would
have enjoyed a more varied diet, richer in calories and the main
nutrients, while expending less energy to obtain it. On the other
hand, with the development of farming techniques, food production
would have been concentrated on cereals which are rich in carbohydrates, more productive and easier to preserve. The quality and
variety of diet, however, would have deteriorated, becoming poorer
and monotonous, while the effort and difficulty required to obtain it
would have been greater. Furthermore, the mortality due to contagious disease would have been intensified by a higher density of
population.[19] The first theory attributes a reduction in mortality to the
demographic acceleration brought about by the development of farming methods. The second theory attributes this rather to an increase
in natural fertility (permanent settlement is more conducive to

reproduction than is the high mobility of a hunting and gathering community) which amply offsets any deterioration in health and mortality. Proofs in favour of one theory or the other are inconclusive, nor can they be otherwise, given the fragmentary nature of the available evidence. It is difficult to give a simple and unequivocal answer to the question of whether the death-rate was higher among hunters and gatherers or among farmers. In favour of the former hypothesis we may adduce the greater irregularity of the food supply and the greater incidence of famine (governed by seasonal and meteorological cycles, for instance) revealed by analyses of bone remains (frequent cases of retarded growth), and also the effects of predation, accidents and violence. In favour of the latter hypothesis are other factors regarding nutrition such as reduced skeletal development in populations that have passed from the pre- to the post-revolutionary phase, the frequency of signs of disease or of bone or dental malformations, and the level of osteoporosis. These elements should be added to the greater incidence of contagious diseases caused by their greater transmissibility in situations of higher population density. Finally, with all the reservations which apply to estimates of mortality based on skeletal remains (problems of their selection, imprecise dating), we cannot prove that the life span of hunters and gatherers was significantly different from that of farmers.

The second food revolution, a short-lived one, coincided with the beginning of the plague cycle in 1348. Demographic decline, lasting roughly a century, made available land that had become so rare at the peak of medieval demographic expansion. Vast tracts formerly under cultivation were converted to pasture. The raising of livestock flourished and the consumption of meat increased greatly.[20] Numerous indicators seem to confirm that in the century prior to the beginning of the modern era, meat consumption reached a level not again attained until the latter part of the previous century or, indeed (as perhaps in Italy), until the present one. Unfortunately, demographic data for the late Middle Ages are rather scanty and do not allow the construction of precise mortality statistics. We do know, however, that the period was marked by recurrent, virulent attacks of the plague at least until the mid-fifteenth century. The ensuing demographic recovery was certainly due more to the attenuation of epidemic crises than to mortality improvements in normal years, the hypothetical consequence of nutritional improvement.

The third food revolution began in the eighteenth century and was the result of a combination of factors which were clearly responsible for a growth in worldwide food resources. These were: the introduction and diffusion of new and productive crops (maize, potatoes); advances in productivity; the cultivation of new land; and a decline in the frequency and severity of famines. It is also the case that during that century, and even more at the beginning of the following one, mortality declined appreciably in many parts of Europe (Great Britain, France, Sweden), and this fact seems to substantiate McKeown's thesis. Also in this case, however, we have no certain proof of a cause-and-effect relationship between these two trends. Indeed many believe that the greater availability of food may have led to population expansion but not to an improvement in nutrition – as in the case of Ireland, for instance – and that in many cases demographic expansion actually had an adverse effect on the quality of nutrition.

There can be no doubt that nutritional variations were of great importance in the history of European populations, nor could it have been otherwise in technologically backward communities which spent the greater part of their resources on food production. But the mechanisms which link demography and nutrition are, to say the least, ambiguous. Simplifying them does not lead to clarity. We shall seek clarity in the chapters that follow.

2

Energy, nutrition and survival

Nutritional requirements

Any discussion of the relationship between survival and nutrition calls for knowledge of certain basic principles, principles which are familiar to anyone dealing with the field of nutrition, but not well known to non-specialists. We must be able to answer the following question: what are, quantitatively and qualitatively, both the basic and the ideal nutritional requirements for survival of the human body? For all its sophistication, this is a question which continues to confound nutritional science. In order to function and therefore survive, the human body needs energy, and this energy is supplied by food. In these pages we shall first discuss human energy requirements and their measurement, and then consider the composition of these requirements in terms of the nutrients essential to healthy survival.

In order that an organism remain healthy it must receive sufficient energy to carry out its normal metabolic functions: to support the processes of growth; to sustain physical activity; to maintain body temperature. Pregnancy and breast-feeding require an additional supplement of energy, just as convalescence after an illness does. Energy requirements vary therefore with age and sex, body weight, state of health, level of physical activity and environmental temperature. In a healthy adult, the intake of energy must equal its expenditure to avoid a wasting of the body tissues caused by calorie deficiency, or an accumulation of fat in the opposite case.[1]

Standards of human caloric requirement are calculated, three of which are summarised in Table 3. As can be seen from this table, the standards vary considerably. For example, the recommended intake for an American male weighing 70 kilos is 2,700 calories a day, while the FAO standard is 3,000 calories for a man weighing 5 kg. less.

23

Table 3 *Three standards of energy requirement (daily caloric intake)*

Population	USA Males	Females	GB Males	Females	FAO Males	Females
Children (1–7 years)	1,300	1,300	1,400	1,300	1,360	1,360
Adolescents[a]	2,800	2,400	2,640	2,150	2,900	2,490
Adults[b]	2,700	2,000	2,900	2,150	3,000	2,200
Elderly[c]	2,400	1,800	2,400	1,800	–	–

[a] USA, 11–14 yrs; GB, 12–14 yrs; FAO, 13–15 yrs
[b] USA, 25–50 yrs; GB, males 18–34 yrs; females 16–54 yrs; FAO n/a
[c] USA, 51 yrs and over; GB, 65–74 yrs
Adult weight: USA, males 70 kg.; females 58 kg.; GB and FAO, males 65 kg.; females 55 kg.
Sources: National Academy of Sciences, *Recommended Daily Allowances* (Washington, 1980); A. E. Bender and D. E. Bender, *Nutrition for Medical Students* (New York, 1982); FAO, *Handbook of Human Nutritional Requirements* (Rome, 1974).

Apart from weight and age, the major source of variation is the degree of physical activity. According to the British standard, the sedentary male requires only 2,500 calories as against the 'very active' male who requires 3,350 calories. The corresponding FAO figures are 2,700 and 3,500. Daily requirements may vary therefore by as much as ten to fifteen per cent around an average, according to the different levels of activity of human groups. Necessary adjustments to external temperature are relatively minor; heavy manual work in a temperature under 14°C, for instance, requires an expenditure of energy five to ten per cent greater than average; similarly, an expenditure of energy above the norm will be required by anyone undertaking heavy physical work at a temperature above 37°C.[2]

The standard values shown in Table 3 are merely for reference and should not be taken as prescriptive. Indeed, individual variation in people of the same sex, age, level of activity and so on is very great. From our own experience we meet people satisfied by vastly different diets, not only in composition but also in caloric value. For individual nutrients (which we shall discuss later in the chapter) the standard values are substantially higher than the arithmetic (theoretical) mean of individual requirements. The American standard, for instance, meets the requirements of the vast majority of the population. But since those requirements are variable – and generally it is assumed that, as for other biological phenomena such as weight and height, a normal curve is adequate to describe the energy requirements of the population – the 'theoretical' arithmetic mean would be insufficient for a large part of the population. Therefore, to satisfy almost everyone, the standard is set at a value twenty per cent above the average requirement.[3] Recommended calorie intake should also exceed what is strictly necessary because of the need for balanced diets which include all the elements essential to healthy survival. This result is obtained through varied diets, and the lower the calorie intake, the harder it is to achieve this variety.

Theoretical nutritional requirements for historical and contemporary
populations

The age and sex structure of a population has a certain influence on its theoretical average nutritional requirement. This can be quite clearly inferred from the lower requirement for children and the elderly compared with that for adults, or for women compared with men. Thus populations with different structures are likely to have different requirements.

Table 4 shows the theoretical average requirements for a range of populations, imagined and real, historical and contemporary. These figures were obtained by applying the standard values summarised in Table 3 to the various populations according to their age and sex distributions. The three theoretical populations represent historically extreme cases; two of these, I and III, are stationary, the former characterised by high fertility and mortality, the latter by low levels of both. The other population, II, is growing as a result of high fertility and low mortality ('low' and 'high', it should be noted, are used relative to historical, rather than present, conditions). Type II has a young age structure and type III a relatively old one. Of the three historical cases, two refer to extreme phases in English demographic history: the end of the seventeenth century when age structure was relatively young, and the beginning of the nineteenth century when it was relatively old. The latter case also resembles that of Tuscany in 1427. The two contemporary examples refer respectively to the more developed and less developed countries, with their well-known differences of structure and demographic dynamics.

As we can see from Table 4, the differences in the theoretical requirement for various populations are not that marked. They exceed 10 per cent only for the FAO 'minimum' (England 1821) and 'maximum' (present-day developed countries), and are little over 5 per cent when considering the US and UK standards ('minimum',

Population and nutrition

Table 4 *Average theoretical caloric requirements for several populations*

| | Theoretical historical cases | | | Actual historical cases | | | Present-day cases 1980 | |
	I	II	III	England 1681	England 1821	Tuscany 1427	more developed countries or MDCs	less developed countries or LDCs
Fertility	High	High	Low	Low	High	High	Low	High
Mortality	High	Low	Low	High	Low	High	Low	Low
Increase	Nil	High	Nil	Neg.	High	Neg.	Low	High
R	2.41	2.71	1.79	1.94	2.98	–	0.98	2.13
e_0	27.9	36.2	36.2	28.5	39.2	–	72.3	57.0
r	0	1.5	0	–0.3	1.5	–	0.7	2.2
% 0–14 years	35.5	38.8	28.6	29.8	39.3	37.2	23.0	39.1
% 60+ years	5.5	5.5	10.0	9.7	6.7	14.6	20.2	6.1
Median age	24	21	28	27	19	21	31.4	20.0
FAO standard	2,392	2,328	2,433	2,426	2,239	2,324	2,484	2,330
US standard	2,187	2,148	2,203	2,181	2,128	2,092	2,233	2,155
GB standard	2,147	2,195	2,272	2,252	2,178	2,153	2,309	2,195

Notes: Models I, II, and III; stable populations (tables by Coale and Demeny), model west; level 3 and r=o; level 8 and r=1.5; level 8 and r=o.

Sources: England 1681 and 1821: E. A. Wrigley and R. Schofield, *The Population History of England 1541–1871* (London, 1981); Tuscany 1427: D. Herlihy and C. Klapisch, *Les Toscans*; more and less developed countries: ONU, 1980.

Tuscany 1427; 'maximum', present-day developed countries). The demographic structure of past populations, it would appear, had at best a secondary effect on energy requirements, and any change in these requirements connected with a change in structure must have taken place very gradually, given the great inertia of demographic phenomena.[4]

As a point of reference, let us calculate what the optimum energy requirement for a historical population might have been, remembering that changes in structure could, with time, cause a degree of fluctuation. If we consider the averages for the three theoretical populations in Table 4, the energy requirements lie between 2,200 and 2,300 calories a day. Assuming substantially lower height and body-weight than is the case today, and partially counterbalancing these with the higher level of physical activity demanded by day-to-day living, we obtain an average of about 2,000 calories. Due to several variations in levels of exertion, this might have varied by plus or minus ten per cent, say 1,800 calories in winter and 2,200 in summer. If we ignore variations in distribution, we can conclude that a population which could rely on a normal consumption of 2,000 calories per head would have been, in centuries past, an adequately fed population, at least from the point of view of energy.[5]

Energy and nutrients

Nutrition experts are only too aware that a diet apparently rich in calories is not necessarily a nutritionally sound diet. Carbohydrates, fats and proteins can all be used by the body as sources of energy. Quantities ingested in excess of the caloric requirement accumulate as fats in adipose tissues. When the calorie intake is low, these reserves of fat are partially drawn upon and converted into energy, a process which causes no damage to the body. Proteins are the source of amino acids, essential to the functional maintenance of the body's tissue. However, should the energy requirement not be met, the proteins accumulated in muscular tissue are 'burned' to make good the calorie deficiency.

A normal diet should contain sufficient quantities of the essential nutrients, namely proteins, vitamins and minerals. Where one or another of these nutrients is deficient, pathological conditions may arise and worsen, no matter how high the calorie intake may be. Recommendations as to the intake of various main nutrients for human populations are continually refined and updated. For example, according to the US standard an adult male who requires 2,700

Table 5 *Nutrient requirements and diseases resulting from their deficiency*

Main nutrients	Daily intake	Main foods containing them	Deficiency-related diseases
Proteins	g.56	Meat, fish, beans (high); cereals (average); vegetables, fruit (low)	Wasting-disease, kwashiorkor
Vitamins Fat soluble			
A	(µg RE) 1000	Meat, fish, beans, milk products, leguminous vegetables	Disturbances of vision, rickets, malformed bones, anaemia
D	(µg) 5	Animal and vegetable fats	Rickets, osteomalacia
E	(mg a-TE)10	Various vegetable foods	Anaemia
Vitamins Water soluble			
C	mg.60	Fruit, greens, liver	Scurvy
Thyamine	mg.1.4	Absent in polished rice	Beri beri, nervous imbalance
Riboflavin	mg.1.6	Wide range of foods	
Niacin	mg.NE 18	Almost absent in maize	Pellagra
Vitamin B6	mg.2.2	Fish, meat	Depression, convulsions
Folic acid	µg 400	Wide range of foods	Anaemia
Vitamin B12	µg 3.0	Meat, eggs, milk products	Pernicious anaemia
Minerals			
Calcium	mg.800	Wide range of foods: milk, beans, cereals (high)	Rickets, osteoporosis
Phosphorus	mg.800	Wide range of foods	Rickets, bone fragility
Magnesium	mg.350	Wide range of foods	Vasodilation, arteriosclerosis

Main nutrients	Daily intake	Main foods containing them	Deficiency-related diseases
Iron	mg.10	Meat, eggs, vegetables, some greens	Anaemia
Zinc	mg.15	Wide range of foods	Dwarfism, retarded growth
Iodine	µg 150	Fish, milk products, many green vegetables	Goitre, cretinism

Note: Average daily requirements for a male adult between the ages of 25 and 50 weighing 70 kg.
Source: National Academy of Sciences, *Recommended Daily Allowances* (Washington, 1980).

calories a day and whose level of activity is average should consume 56 grams of protein together with specified quantities of vitamins and minerals. Table 5 gives a summary of the recommended daily allowances of the various nutrients, together with lists of the foods containing them and the pathologies which can arise in their absence. It should be pointed out, however, that these recommended allowances tend to change, not only due to the continuous broadening of scientific knowledge but also as a result of the life style and consumption habits of a population. The British standard recommended intake is 69 grams of protein as compared with the US recommendation of 56 grams.[6] This discrepancy probably reflects an incomplete understanding of the precise relationship between nutrition, health and sickness.

Despite this uncertainty, which is compounded when confronting historical examples, many associations are well-known. Lack of protein – high concentrations of which are present in animal foods, such as meat or fish, but also in vegetables like beans – causes the terrible diseases of infancy which lie at the root of the high mortality in developing countries: marasmus (wasting disease) and kwashiorkor. A dearth of vitamin A is responsible for blindness, of vitamin D – contained in animal and vegetable fats – for rickets, and of vitamin C, for scurvy, once the scourge of ships' crews the world over; while a lack of niacin was at the root of the pellagra which spread over a good part of southern Europe in the eighteenth and nineteenth centuries. Among the minerals, a deficiency of calcium and phosphorus can lead to rickets and bone malformations, while iodine deficiency can lead to goitre and cretinism, conditions once prevalent in mountain areas, such as the Pyrenees, Alps and Carpathians.[7]

An analysis of nutrient requirements and the consequences of their absence would be a sterile exercise in this context, particularly in view of the general lack of information on the composition of diets in the past. It is important to stress, however, that all the nutrients essential to healthy survival can be found in a large variety of products which are consumed across a very broad cultural, climatic and economic spectrum, and that a satisfactory diet is obtainable more or less anywhere. For example, foods of animal origin like meat, fish and eggs contain high quality proteins, but cereals and leguminous vegetables also contain proteins, and these in combination can provide an adequate diet, even where animal proteins are absent.[8] Traditional Mediterranean and Mesoamerican diets, rich in leguminous vegetables and cereals, are quite adequate in terms of proteins, and whole populations who live on strictly vegetarian diets show no evidence of protein deficiency.

Clear distortions do exist in certain diets, especially where extreme climatic conditions prevail (for instance very cold marginal lands) or in particular social contexts (scurvy among ships' crews), or in periods of famine and social upheaval. In these circumstances, deficiency may become chronic and the natural process of adaptation between man and nutritional resources negated or blocked. Another point, which I intend to expand upon later, relates to the physiological capacity of the human species to adapt to levels of nutrition considered deficient or inadequate, by abstract standards.[9] This capacity may be greater than is generally admitted, due to processes of adaptation and selection developed by mankind during its long history.

To be sure, the nature of diets in the past is not entirely unknown, in spite of the rarity of quantitative data. Table 6 and Figures 6 and 7 show the breakdown of caloric intake by origin and composition in France and Italy.[10] Of course, for the earlier years, poor in reliable statistics, any estimates are bound to be little more than indications. Nonetheless temporal evolution reveals clearly the changes in diet that have taken place in the modern age. With time, calorie supply has increased markedly (even allowing for the fact that it has been underestimated for France at the end of the *ancien régime,* as we shall see) while the proportion of calories derived from carbohydrates has declined and that derived from fats increased (though this tendency

Table 6 *Per capita daily calorie supply by origin and composition in France and Italy, eighteenth to twentieth centuries*

	1781–90 France	1861–70 France	1861–70 Italy	1961–70 France	1961–70 Italy
		Animal or vegetable origin			
Total calories	1,753	2,875	2,628	3,309	2,897
Animal	293	478	266	1,494	511
Vegetable	1,460	2,397	2,362	1,815	2,386
		Composition percent			
Total calories	100	100	100	100	100
Animal	17	17	10	45	18
Vegetable	83	83	90	55	82
		Composition by nutrient			
Total calories	1,753	2,875	2,628	3,309	2,897
Protein	208	360	346	378	342
Fat	288	504	564	1,422	804
Carbohydrates	1,257	2,011	1,718	1,509	1,751
		Composition per cent			
Total calories	100	100	100	100	100
Protein	11.9	12.5	13.2	11.4	11.8
Fat	16.4	17.5	21.5	43.0	27.8
Carbohydrates	71.7	70.0	65.3	45.6	60.4

Sources: France: J.-C. Toutain, 'La consommation alimentaire en France de 1789 à 1964', *Economie et Société*, Cahier de l'ISEA, vol. A, no. 11 (Geneva, 1971); Italy: ISTAT, *Statistiche storiche dell'Italia 1861–1975* (Rome, 1976). Data for France refer to 1865–74 and 1965–6 as well as 1861–70 and 1961–70.

is rather less pronounced in Italy). If we examine the sources – vegetable or animal – of calories, we see that the proportion of calories of animal origin has increased, strongly in France, less so in Italy. This is true for proteins and especially for fats. In France, fats once chiefly of vegetable origin now derive primarily from animals. If we classify present-day countries according to income, we observe not only that calorie supply grows with income, but also that the incidence of calories from animals, richer in both protein and fat, increases as well. Yet, within the range of these general tendencies, wide variations

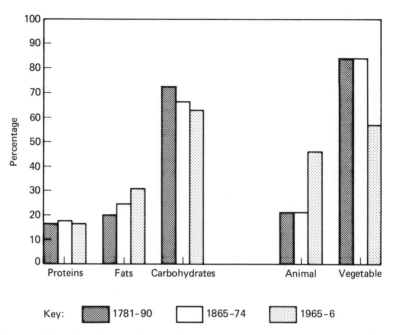

Figure 6 Calorie supply in France by composition and source, eighteenth to twentieth centuries
Source: J.-C. Toutain, 'La consommation alimentaire en France de 1789 à 1964', *Economie et Société*, Cahier de l'ISEA, vol. A, no. 11 (Geneva, 1971).

may occur between populations even at the same income level. In Japan, for instance, calories derived from fats represent barely ten per cent of the total intake, compared to more than forty per cent in many Western countries. Furthermore we shall see that other noticeable transformations have occurred in the past connected, for example, with the decline of meat consumption at the start of the modern era.

Nutrition and mortality

A rich biomedical literature confirms the dictates of common sense, namely, that a close relationship does exist between levels of nutrition, infectious disease, and their severity. Generally speaking, we can say that a poorly nourished population is more susceptible to infectious diseases and less able to combat their spread, severity and outcome. Again in general terms, we can maintain that, given a population subject to the high mortality of the past, the transition from a state of malnutrition to one of adequate nutrition and vice

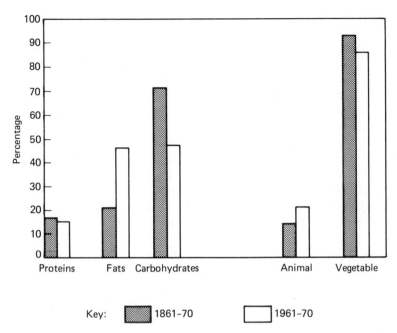

Figure 7 Calorie supply in Italy by composition and source, nineteenth to twentieth centuries
Source: ISTAT, *Statistiche storiche dell'Italia, 1861-1975* (Rome, 1976).

versa – due, for example, to variations in farming productivity – can determine analogous changes in the level of mortality.[11] Unacceptable, however, is a third generalisation that assumes the existence of an inverse relationship between nutritional levels on the one hand, and infection and mortality on the other. Indeed, such a relation is absent beyond the thin line which divides malnutrition from adequate nutrition, and becomes actually positive in the case of hypernutrition.

The logic of this study requires the clarification of several points. The first concerns the nature of the relationship between nutrition and disease. The vast body of scientific literature is quite clear on the matter, as we shall see. The second concerns the identification of that nutritional threshold below which the chances of survival start to decline. There is much controversy and doubt about this matter, if only for the difficulty of defining satisfactorily the nutritional levels of individuals and communities. The third issue concerns the identification of those populations which, in different historical periods, have crossed that danger threshold in one direction or the other, and the demographic consequences of this passage. This third point is at the heart of our work and is the main concern of the coming chapters.

The interaction between malnutrition and contagious disease is generally viewed in terms of a lowering of the body's defences which stimulates the incidence, spread, gravity and outcome of the infection. This is not to say that the effect of nutrition on other pathologies does not exist (relationships to which we referred in the previous section). On the contrary, the high mortality of the past was due primarily to infectious diseases, and its reduction came about as a result of their control. It is therefore legitimate to concentrate on the relationship between nutrition and infection. In particular, inadequate nutrition is thought to exercise a negative influence on a range of the organism's natural defences. These include both the specific responses of the immunological system (the action of the immunoglobins and antibodies, lymphocytes and so forth), with their antitoxic, antibacterial, antiviral and antiparasitical functions, as well as the so-called non-specific factors of resistance (such as phagocyte activity, the health of the skin and mucous membranes, important points of entry for many infections) to bacterial attack and infections in general.[12]

In a work which has rightly remained famous, Scrimshaw and others have analysed hundreds of studies on the relationship between infectious disease and malnutrition in numerous populations. They reach the conclusion that malnutrition exacerbates the greater part of infectious processes by a synergic effect, and only in a minority of cases does the incidence of infection not increase.[13] However, this conclusion, which as a first approximation is shared by all, calls for closer inspection as it is more ambiguous than it at first appears. The considerations to be made are three:

1 In an overwhelming majority of the studies in question, malnutrition is always associated with poverty, ignorance, unfavourable environmental and hygienic conditions, all factors which have an important influence, whether direct or indirect, on the incidence, spread and outcome of many diseases. It is almost always impossible to determine the 'net' influence of malnutrition on disease, and the association perceived is often spurious. One recent survey of studies on infancy reached the conclusion that the high frequency of infection in children who suffer from mild or average malnutrition was linked more to the quality of the environment than to the level of nutrition.[14]

2 The measurement of levels of nutrition present another difficult

problem. It is almost impossible, in large-scale studies, to carry out direct observations on levels of food consumption. As a substitute, simple anthropometric measurements are often used.[15] For example, a weight-to-age parameter is often used for children whose deviation from a pre-set standard is taken as an index of mild, average or serious undernutrition.[16] For adults, the weight–height relationship or other anthropometric measurements (circumference of the forearm, skin fold thickness, and so on) are used and then measured against a reference standard. These measurements are naturally imperfect, in part because they fail to take individual variation into account.

3 The existence of an infectious process inhibits the absorption of essential nutrients, thus aggravating the state of malnutrition.[17] Malnutrition thus becomes the effect, rather than the cause, of an infectious process (brought on, for instance, by autonomous environmental factors). It is well known, for example, that diarrhoea, one of the most widespread infections occurring in developing countries and a principal cause of infant mortality, reduces the individual's ability to take in and absorb food and is in itself therefore a major cause of malnutrition.[18]

The circumstances are such as to make it difficult to measure the relationship between nutrition and mortality, both because of the close interaction between these two phenomena and because of their indissoluble link with economic and environmental conditions. Yet even assuming we were able to overcome these difficulties, other considerations arise to complicate an issue that at first sight seemed simple.

Nutrition and infection: a controversial association

Before concluding this incursion into the biomedical field, there are other aspects of the nutrition–infection relationship to be confronted which further complicate the picture. It is indispensable to understand whether there exists a threshold of malnutrition beyond which the risk of infection increases sharply, and it is also important to understand whether all infectious processes are sensitive to the level of food intake or if there are some exceptions.

I have already discussed the difficulties involved in measuring nutritional levels. I shall mention in passing that experimental studies with animals, the only sort which allow one to study the effects of a precisely graduated food intake, have resulted in controversial findings, findings which at any rate cannot be easily extended to the human species.[19] The Canalis and Morpurgo experiment on mice and pigeons, known for their natural resistance to the anthrax bacillus, has gone down in the annals of medical history.[20] When subjected to starvation and artificially infected by the anthrax bacillus, the mice did not show any particular reaction, whereas all the pigeons died. But animals apart, what can be said about the functional relation between level of nutrition, incidence of infection and mortality? Apparently the relation is non-existent when the infection is either very mild or very virulent: for instance, the common cold or the plague.

Recently, a survey of studies in Colombia, India, Nepal and Bangladesh has highlighted how, in the first years of life, clinical measures of cellular immunity (CMI) show consistently lower levels in undernourished children than in normally-fed children.[21] However, this is not evidence enough, because the minimum immune response needed to ward off infection and disease is an unknown quantity. As far as the onset of respiratory and intestinal infections is concerned, there are no noteworthy differences connected with nutritional state, whereas duration, and therefore severity, are perceptibly greater among the malnourished. If we observe mortality as a function of nutrition, we notice that risk of death is substantially higher for children in a severe state of malnutrition, while differences in mortality between 'moderately' and 'slightly' undernourished children are uncertain or weak.[22] The results of the Bangladeshi and Indian studies are shown in Figure 8. In the first case, the nutrition-mortality relationship reveals a threshold: there is a marked increase in mortality only for the severely undernourished. In the second case the relationship is curvilinear: the curve takes a sudden upward turn as malnutrition passes from slight to moderate.

Having in some measure thrown light on the link between malnutrition and mortality, we may now add other elements to complete this survey. Not all infectious diseases are 'sensitive' in the sense employed thus far to malnutrition. Indeed nutritional deficiencies, if they can depress the human body's defences, can also in certain cases interfere with the metabolic and reproductive processes of the attacking micro-organism. In some cases malnutrition has an antagonistic, rather than a synergic, effect, thus limiting the damage done by infection. While the action of bacterial infections is almost always synergic, that of viral diseases is often as antagonistic as synergic. Parasitical infections would appear to lie half-way between the bacterial and the viral.[23] If we consider the main forms of infection, we can recognise that for many of those which played a decisive

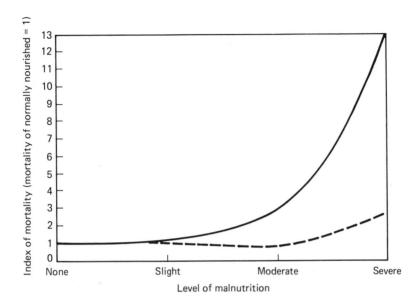

Figure 8 Malnutrition and mortality
Source: Adapted from R. Martorell and T. J. Ho.

role in determining historical levels of mortality, the connection with nutrition seems minimal or non-existent. Table 7 provides some examples. From it we can infer that nutritional deficiency had little or no responsibility for the effects of the plague, smallpox or malaria. It did have considerable responsibility, however, for the effects of many types of intestinal and respiratory illness, while remaining indeterminate or variable for other important diseases such as typhus and diphtheria.[24]

Estimating the repercussions of varying nutritional levels on infection and the death-rate in past times is, to say the least, problematic. Certainly, periods of severe undernutrition could not have failed to have consequences for survival, especially in young children whose organisms require a high energy input for development.

It is still true today that childhood is most likely to be adversely affected by calorie or protein deficiency, which gives rise in so many developing countries to such diseases as marasmus and kwashiorkor.[25] These are further aggravated not only by the harmful effects of

Table 7 *Influence of nutritional level on certain infective processes*

Clear influence	Influence uncertain, variable	Influence minimal, non-existent
Cholera	Diphtheria	Encephalitis
Diarrhoea	Helminthiasis/worms	Yellow fever
Herpes	Staphylococcus infection	Malaria
Leprosy	Streptococcus infection	Plague
Respiratory diseases	Influenza	Tetanus
Measles	Syphilis	Typhoid
Intestinal parasites	Typhus	Smallpox
Whooping cough		
Tuberculosis		

Source: 'The Relationship of Nutrition, Disease and Social Conditions: a Graphical Presentation', in R. I. Rotberg and T. K. Rabb (eds.), *Hunger and History* (Cambridge, Mass., Harvard University Press, 1985), p. 308.

poverty, but also by other factors specific to our times, above all reduced or insufficient breast-feeding which when adequate provides efficient defences during a large part of the first year of life, and also the inadequacy of substitute nourishment.[26]

Among the infections whose relationship with nourishment is uncertain or variable (see Table 7) we can count many cases in which it is hard to extrapolate to the past from the results of recent observations. It is plausible, for instance, that a state of undernourishment may exacerbate the effect of typhus, but recent experience is, at the very least, contradictory. Russian prisoners at Hammerstein camp, for example, suffered a notably lower death-rate than their German guards.[27] Also contradictory was the experience of the great influenza epidemic of 1918–19 which, according to many contemporaries, seemed to be totally disconnected from the nutritional state of the populations affected.[28] The link between the incidence of respiratory illnesses and the level of nourishment would also appear to be contradictory.

This survey of the relationship between nutrition and infectious diseases has undoubtedly gone some way towards shaking certain assumptions which population historians have taken for granted.

We may agree that malnutrition does play its part in worsening the conditions of survival in the presence of other factors which favour the spreading of infections and act against their cessation (poor hygiene, poverty, ignorance). But in assessing the net effect, the role of malnutrition is not uniform, being nil for some diseases, uncertain and variable for others, considerable and certain for still others. In relation to some pathologies, undernourishment seems to act antagonistically and so beneficially. One authority has even stated that 'there is some evidence in support of the thesis that calculated mild undernutrition and leanness may be an animal's greatest physical asset, producing longer life, fewer malignancies, reduced mortality from inherited susceptibility to auto-immune disease and perhaps fewer infections'.[29] Even without entirely endorsing this opinion, it is plausible to maintain that above certain specific levels of malnutrition, individual organic defences are not weakened. Identifying these levels, or 'danger thresholds' as I have called them above, and ascertaining the distribution of the population in relation to these, a task already difficult for the demographer equipped with modern data, is perhaps an impossible one for the historian of past populations.

3

Famine and want

Starvation and survival: clinical and historical cases

What happens to the human organism when its intake of food is reduced, it crosses the critical threshold of malnutrition and stays below it for a shorter or longer, but transitory, amount of time? Passing from individual or clinical case histories to the experiences of entire communities, what happens to a population that through want, war or some other catastrophe has to survive for a lengthy period with food availability clearly below what is considered adequate?

The lessons that can be learned from clinical and historical cases about the relationship between short-term nutritional stress and survival will be the object of this chapter. The assumption is that by studying cases that are extreme but neither abnormal nor infrequent in the past, we may gain a better insight into the mechanisms of resistance and adaptability in the face of food shortage.

The human body has developed a degree of adaptability to a lack of food. A fast lasting the biblical forty days and forty nights is well within reach of any healthy adult and should not entail, providing the subsequent return to an adequate diet, any long-term adverse effects.[1] Many interpret this resistance as the consequence of a long selection process taking place over hundreds of thousands of years during which man, or his precursors, lived by hunting and gathering in unstable environments, subject to recurring periods of scarcity. Thus the capacity to accumulate fat may have developed as a survival mechanism in times of perhaps seasonally but at any rate recurrent dearth. It is thought that the tendency of Polynesians to accumulate fat is a consequence of a selection process taking place during the long sea-journeys undertaken to populate distant and scattered islands in the archipelago, a process analogous to the accumulation of fat in hibernating bears or migrating birds.[2]

Individual and well-documented cases of long resistance to complete food deprivation are numerous and provide a fund of dismal anecdote. Almost by chance, I came upon the documented account by a doctor of the avalanche which, on 19 March 1755, buried the greater part of the houses in the village of Bergemoletto in upper Val di Stura, Italy: three women buried alive in a stable were freed thirty-seven days later during the thaw.[3] Not by coincidence, it was in the eighteenth century that learned debate was launched on the ability to survive for long periods in a state of complete starvation without jeopardising health. Even the future Pope Benedict XIV was involved in the debate. Leaving aside the stories of hermits and visionaries, victims of earthquake or shipwreck, charlatans and fakirs which have populated sensationalist literature past and present, I shall recall two tragic and well-documented historical cases. In 1920, the Irish nationalist Mac Swiney, mayor of Cork, survived in prison for seventy-four days before dying of starvation.[4] Sixty years later, between March and August of 1981, ten young Irish nationalists, headed by Bobby Sands, starved to death in prison surviving without taking food for forty-five to seventy-three days.[5]

In the context of this book, occasional instances of total lack of food are not very interesting, since it is not my purpose to explore the outer limits of endurance, but only the relative ones such as would often be reached in past centuries during periods of famine.

The deservedly most famous of all experimental clinical studies is that carried out by Ancel Keys and his colleagues at the University of Minnesota during the 1940s on a group of thirty-two young conscientious objectors.[6] These volunteers lived for a year at the Laboratory of Physiological Hygiene. Their stay was divided into a three month term of normal but monitored diet and activity, followed by six months of semi-fasting and a final three months for rehabilitation and control. During the three initial months they received a substantial diet of 3,492 calories a day; during the six months of half-fasting their daily caloric intake was reduced to 1,570 calories a day supplied by cabbages, turnips and potatoes, with only a few grams of animal protein added per week. 'At the end of six months on this diet the subjects had lost twenty-four per cent of their body weight and showed the classical signs and symptoms of famine victims, namely edema, anaemia, polyuria, bradycardia, weakness and depression.'[7]

During the half-fast, a regular and complex series of clinical observations was carried out on the subjects of the experiment. Many interesting conclusions were drawn from these analyses about the mechanisms of adaptation to such an exceptional situation. The rate of weight-loss decreased weekly, settling at around 0.13 kg. during the last three weeks. In other words, the energy released for use by the organism – beyond the 1,570 calories of the diet – 'burning', so to speak, the body's capital of fats and body tissue, reached a minimum during the closing phases of the experiment. These young men, while suffering various symptoms, nevertheless managed to exist in a state of relative energy equilibrium, consuming fifty-five per cent less than the normal number of calories. How was this saving achieved? The energy requirement for basic metabolism (the energy consumption of the body in a state of repose, as in sleep), estimated at 1,576 calories normally, was reduced at the end of the experiment to 962 calories (minus thirty-nine per cent), essentially due to a drop in body weight. A large part of the residual reduction in energy requirement was attributed to a reduction in non-essential physical activity (that is not connected with specifically irreducible actions such as getting dressed, washing, minimum indispensable movement and so on), passing from a consumption of 1,567 calories to barely 451 (minus seventy-two per cent). Of this further reduction by 1,116 calories forty per cent was attributed by the researchers to reduced body weight (in other words, for every action the quantity of energy consumed was lower in direct proportion to the reduced body weight) and sixty per cent to effective reduction of physical activity to a minimum. Table 8 summarises the results of this experiment.

Finally, among the many results of the study, one of particular interest for the purposes of the topic under discussion was the discovery of a very low incidence of respiratory infections in the subjects, although they continued normal social contact.[8]

The Minnesota experiment is important because it confirms the existence of 'protective' mechanisms in the event of nutritional stress. These mechanisms operate by reducing, within physiological bounds, the daily energy requirement of the organism. A reduction in body weight (provided of course it does not reach the point of irreversible damage) leads to a considerable reduction of this requirement. A reduction in non-essential physical activity produces a further saving. These adjustments were sufficient to enable our volunteers to survive with their energy consumption reduced by fifty-five per cent while experiencing a considerably smaller reduction in body weight. Naturally, this adaptability took its toll (quite apart from the effects described above), particularly in the form of an acute sense of weakness.

Table 8 *Energy consumption of thirty-two young men before and after six months of semi-starvation*

Energy consumption (kCal)	Before	After	Absolute difference	Percentage difference
Basic metabolism	1,576	962	614	39
Specific activities	349	157	192	55
Reducible activities	1,567	451	1,116	72
Total	3,492	1,570	1,922	55
Body weight (kg.)	69.4	52.6	16.8	24

Source: H. L. Taylor and A. Keys, 'Adaptation to Caloric Restriction', *Science*, 112, August 1950.

Keys' results have been confirmed by other studies,[9] even though no later investigation has achieved the precision and accuracy of the Minnesota experiment. Nonetheless, however accurate, these results do relate to young, healthy individuals in a healthy, controlled environment and under the constant surveillance of a team of doctors working within the parameters of an experiment of prescribed duration, an experiment which could have been suspended at any moment. Also, the reduced diet, though meagre, contained essential nutrients and the subjects of the experiment, unhampered by commitments, were able to reduce their activities to a bare minimum. Such conditions are patently different from those of populations who, suffering famine, also lack medical aid, have to endure harsh environmental conditions, are characterised by a high proportion of vulnerable individuals (children, the elderly, the sick), and often consume unbalanced diets. Besides experiencing the psychological stress associated with such dangerous situations, these populations are also constrained to expend huge amounts of energy to obtain food. It is to populations such as these, therefore, that we must turn to obtain more realistic data, at the cost, however, of less precise and detailed results and the difficulty of unravelling the web of factors unfavourable to survival.

Three cases of starving populations in our own century

The further back we go in time, the more difficult it becomes to sort out the plethora of factors that determine mortality increase in a population. Certain events in the history of the present century, involving large-scale famine in whole populations during the two

World Wars, merit consideration. I shall pass over the numerous incidences of hunger suffered by prisoners or internees in concentration camps. The unusual selection of these groups and the generally poor accuracy of the empirical observations made, render a large number of examples virtually unusable. I shall also exclude examples offered by modern famines – in India, Bangladesh, Ethiopia or Sahel – even though they have been accurately documented, as they belong to social and geographical contexts which are remote from our purposes. I shall therefore limit myself to three instances: to the Venetian territories the year after the defeat at Caporetto (October 1917–October 1918); to the populations of western Holland during the winter 1944–5; and to the Warsaw ghetto in 1941– 2.

After the defeat at Caporetto and until the battle of Vittorio Veneto, a period of precisely one year, roughly 12,500 km^2 belonging to the provinces of Treviso, Venice and Vicenza, with slightly less than one million inhabitants, were occupied by the Austrians.[10] According to Mortara's calculations, the death-rate rose during that year from a pre-war average (1912–14) of 14.8 per thousand to 44.9 per thousand, a threefold increase. In addition to the upheavals caused by the invasion, by forced evictions, by the deportation of numerous contingents of men, and by the lack of doctors and medicines, the rise in the death-rate is certainly connected with conditions of famine. The resources and provisions available at the time of the defeat at Caporetto were to a large extent confiscated to supply the Austrian troops. The same fate awaited the cereal harvest of 1918. Official rations of maize flour were reduced in December to 150 grams and later to 100 grams. Meat rations of 200 grams per week were purely theoretical given the total lack of livestock. In January 1918, confiscation by the occupying forces extended to almost all foodstuffs. 'Essentially, for several months, from February to the middle of 1918, over half the occupied region was reduced to daily rations of less than 100 grams of maize flour.'[11]

The systematic plundering of the food resources in this region is well documented, and had it not been for the small reserves which the population was able to hide here and there, particularly in the country, official rationing would undoubtedly have resulted in the death of a far larger section of the population than it did. The consequences of famine in this large area were not slow in making themselves felt; hydroemia, dropsy and dysentery spread everywhere, as health reports and other witnesses' accounts testify. The Royal Commission reckoned that 9,747 people died 'of hunger', 22.4 per cent of the total death toll. This datum is, of course, approximate, given the difficulty of distinguishing deaths for which famine is the prime cause from those for which it was merely a concomitant cause. We should add, however, that observers noted the extremely low impact of the influenza epidemic, rampant in unoccupied Italy, and no serious epidemics were reported. In short, it was famine, without much help from outside factors, which was the prime and direct cause of the rise in mortality.

The winter of 1944–5 in Holland provides another famous and tragic case. Under Nazi occupation the west of the country, including Amsterdam, The Hague and Rotterdam, found itself utterly cut-off and bereft of supplies from the Allied advance on the Rhine in November 1944 until the liberation on 7 May 1945.[12] The calorie supply per capita, obtained as far as possible from charity contributions, black market purchases and the problematic and risky provisions obtained from the surrounding countryside, was 1,876 calories in Amsterdam in October 1944, dropping to 1,290 in February 1945 and then again to 1,243 by the following April. The clinical symptoms of malnutrition (edema) were frequent and serious. Hospitals could not cope with the numbers of patients and many schools had to be turned into hospitals. We get some idea of the severity of the situation if we bear in mind that, initially, food supplements were issued to the sick who had lost twenty-five per cent of their body weight, but later, due to the increasing numbers of people in this condition, the weight loss criterion was raised to thirty-five per cent. The supplement to the official daily ration of 670 calories was 400 grams of bread (in March and April). It was estimated that starvation edema affected about ten per cent of the population, which on average had lost fifteen to twenty per cent in body weight. Starvation hit the cities more than the countryside. In The Hague, between January and April, the numbers of deaths increased by 134 per cent compared with the same period the preceding year. If we exclude deaths directly attributable to the effects of war, the increase was 111 per cent, three-quarters of which were attributed directly to the consequences of starvation. If we take all twelve of Holland's western cities, the number of deaths grew from 13,155 to 29,122 (plus 121 per cent) between the early months of 1944 and the early months of 1945.

The third case, certainly the most tragic, is that of the Warsaw ghetto, which for over a year and a half – until 22 July 1942, the date of the onset of mass deportations and systematic gas chamber annihilations of over 250,000 surviving Jews – was virtually walled in by the Nazis and cut off from the outside world, forced to survive on existing stocks and on what the ingenuity and courage born of despair could smuggle in from the outside world.[13] In that ghetto, a whole population had to live for a long period on minimal resources. In the two hospitals, a team of heroic doctors carried out clinical investigations on a large number of 'normal' patients, during the last months, when the average calorie supply was 800 calories a day per head. The number of deaths, already 8,981 in the troubled year of 1940, rose to 43,239 in 1941 and 29,788 during the first seven months of 1942. Typhus, virtually endemic, killed 216 people in 1940, 1,991 in 1941 and 512 during the first seven months of 1942; starvation killed 91, 10,971 and 7,254 respectively. In 1941, and during the first seven months of 1942, deaths directly attributable to starvation amounted to about a quarter of the total deceased.

These three fairly detailed cases, sadly drawn from a long history of collective tragedy,[14] prompt two observations. The first concerns the relatively low incidence of epidemic phenomena. I have already drawn attention to the low level of influenza pandemia in the occupied territories of the Veneto during the First World War. Cowell noted that this disease seemed to affect indiscriminately both well-fed troops and poorly-fed populations.[15] Observations made in prisoner of war camps in Germany and Japan,[16] while showing an increase in intestinal infections, verified surprisingly low levels for other infections. In the Warsaw ghetto, apart from typhus, which actually diminished in 1942 when starvation reached its peak, doctors were amazed at the relatively low incidence of epidemic attack and infection in general.[17] During the Minnesota experiments, as I have said, cases of respiratory infection were relatively low during the period of semi-fasting.

The second observation is closely linked to the first. In the three cases reported above, notwithstanding increases in the death-rate, which doubled in Holland during periods of crisis, tripled in the Veneto and quadrupled or quintupled in the Warsaw ghetto, the number of deaths due 'directly' to starvation was very high and numbered a quarter or a third of all deaths. If the link between lack of food and infection were close and inevitable (as it is, for instance, in the case of tuberculosis), gradual starvation would not lead directly to death, as infection would overtake starvation as the cause of death. This should be all the more true when populations are exposed to all manner of contagion, a condition exacerbated by the hazards of war, enemy occupation or siege. In communities, then, hunger and starvation are linked to increased mortality not only, nor even primarily, because of lowered resistance, but also, and in far greater measure, because of the increased 'transmissibility' of infections resulting from upsets in the social order, overcrowding and a worsening of hygienic and environmental conditions. In those cases where social organisation, though sorely tried, nonetheless survives, increased mortality is imputable above all to the 'direct and final' consequences of starvation rather than to epidemic attacks.[18] This is the lesson to be drawn from the three cases discussed.[19]

Clinical–experimental studies, and studies of modern populations subjected to serious nutritional stress, point, therefore, to two conclusions.[20] In the first place they highlight the physiological limitations of the adaptability to nutritional stress. As we have seen, this adaptation takes the form of a reduction in the energy requirement due to a loss of body weight and a reduction in non-essential body activity.[21] Naturally this process has its limits, but it allows people to carry on for several months at varying levels of efficiency without altogether compromising their chances of survival. It may be sufficient, in many cases, to live through a siege, wait for help to arrive or get through to the next harvest.

The second conclusion is that the link between starvation and infection is, to a large extent, a spurious one. As we saw in chapter 2, malnutrition weakens certain organic defences but leaves others unscathed. If pushed to the limits of human survival, it can kill without the intervention of infectious disease. The long recognised and accepted link between want and epidemic attacks, which we shall study in more detail below, can often be attributed to the creation of particular social conditions which increase the transmissibility of infectious disease more than directly stimulating their incidence.

Subsistence crises and mortality in the pre-industrial age

'City fathers, take pity on us, show charity, and give us grain for the love of God, that we may not die of hunger, we and our families.' How often has this plea, directed at Florentine officials by suppliants left in the squares without bread during the famine of 1329, been repeated?[22] History abounds with stories of this kind and they could easily fill volumes. Want was a familiar presence in Europe, from which no generation escaped. Indeed a single lifetime might see its repeated occurrence. It is from these recurring collective experiences of nutritional stress that we can cull valuable information on the relationship between food and mortality.

Quantitative history, economic, demographic and social, often teaches us more about the short term than the long. We shall see in the following sections how difficult it is to trace, even summarily, modes and levels of nutrition over centuries. On the other hand, the study of oscillations in food availability over short periods presents less of a problem. In fact, there exists a rich documentation on harvests, famines and their economic, demographic and social consequences. In particular, the comparison between the price series for large consumption staples and that for deaths enables us to examine systematically the relationship between short-term fluctuations of both. Jean Meuvret drew the attention of demographers to this in 1946, maintaining that the systematic analysis of a relationship well-known and well-understood by contemporaries, and facilitated by the availability of long historical series, could be very revealing.[23]

The logical chain is as follows. Pre-industrial European populations were, for the most part, consumers of cereals which, in the form of bread, loaves, buns, porridge and so forth, constituted the staple diet of the large majority of the population. When the harvest failed, usually for climatic reasons, prices rose and anyone who needed to purchase flour or bread in order to satisfy dietary needs saw his purchasing power drastically reduced, and in extreme cases had to go without. Often one could avoid scarcity by substituting inferior for high quality grain, but if the year was particularly bad, all grain types would be affected indiscriminately. For many, reduced food availability meant a weakening of the organism and eventually death from starvation, or, more frequently, from epidemic infection.

A sudden rise in prices would therefore be followed by a rise in mortality. Of course, dearth also brought other demographically serious consequences in its wake, such as a drop in marriages and conceptions and, almost always, a great increase in the number of wandering and hungry beggars, a phenomenon characteristic of the onset of epidemic cycles.[24]

Some links in this otherwise strong chain of reasoning are not unassailable. In the first place, while price trends reflected the market value of wheat or other cereal, we do not know what portion of each family's food resources was purchased on the market and what portion was directly produced and consumed or bartered or received in exchange for services or labour. Braudel has estimated that in the sixteenth and seventeenth centuries only two to three per cent of Europe's cereal consumption came from international trade,[25] but we know nothing about what total share of production reached the market.

Let us imagine that the annual production of cereals is divided into two quotas: the first intended for home consumption, or in any case not reaching the market, the second for sale. Now, it may be that a reduction in availability would affect the first quota less than proportionally and affect the second more than proportionally. We may also assume that the larger the home consumption quota the weaker the relationship will be between fluctuations in price and fluctuations in consumption, and so in mortality. It should also be noted that communities enjoying a greater variety of resources or a lower density of population, or abounding in more common land, suffer less from the consequences of one or more years of agricultural failure.

All in all, in the light of our discussion up to now, the onset of an epidemic could be caused more by the social than by the bionatural consequences of a famine. Famine, we know, increased disproportionately the already conspicuous mass of beggars and vagrants. It swelled the numbers migrating to towns, it packed the poorhouses, hospices and hospitals, it made easier the spread of epidemic diseases such as typhus.[26] A contemporary witness of a famine, Giovanni Battista Segni in Bologna in 1602,[27] 'would hear the whole populace cry out, would see the people justly revolt, the poor rend the air with their wailings, the countryfolk exclaim till their lungs might burst, the hospitals fill up, the droning of wretched voices at the doors of the rich, the squares in an uproar, the foodstores and stalls swarming with distressed and wretched people': an ideal situation for the outbreak and spread of an epidemic, usually typhus. In the last great famine of the West, the Irish Famine which began in 1845, typhus, known as the 'famine fever', caused a large proportion of the deaths.

The circumstances were ideal for lice and for those micro-organisms, agents of typhus, transmitted by lice. The extent of nutrition in individuals did not seem to affect the vulnerability to typhus, as demonstrated by the large number of voluntary workers – doctors, priests, nuns, government officials and others – who contracted the disease and died of it. The 'famine fever' was then transmitted across the Atlantic to Canada and the United States by the miserable fugitives from famine.[28]

With regard to the mortality differential caused by famine fever, I think it worthwhile to quote a contemporary report: 'The mortality among the better class was truly great, six or seven out of ten dying of it, while among the poor who got no care at all, not more than one out of every four or five attacked was carried off by it.'[29]

One is inclined to ask the following question: was the increased mortality caused by epidemic factors connected with undernourishment or not?[30] The question may seem an unprofitable one since the general coincidence between famine and mortality is well-proven as we shall see. Why should we concern ourselves with whether an epidemic attack was brought about by social conditions favouring contagion or by undernourishment? And, in any case, how are we going to separate the two components?

Though the question may seem to serve no purpose, in reality it does, at least from a theoretical point of view. Its solution will determine how short-term observations may be used to explain events in the long term. For if famine leads to undernourishment which in turn increases the risk of epidemic disease, then it can be argued that in the long run, a slight but continuous impoverishment of diet would automatically result in a worsening of mortality in normal periods and a rise in the frequency of epidemics. If, on the other hand, the coincidence between subsistence crises and mortality is due to the biosocial circuit, then the hypothesis, while not invalidated, loses much of its exploratory strength.

A brief chronology of European famines

The chronology of Europe's great food crises, in large part ascribable to climatic factors, is fairly well-known in outline. Furthermore, series of deaths and prices, available with some frequency from the sixteenth century onwards, allow us to establish the quantitative links between the two phenomena. Not that there is a lack of information for the preceding centuries – we only have to think about the severe subsistence crisis that afflicted most of Europe in the second decade of the fourteenth century[31] – but the lack of reliable series for deaths and the regularly recurring action of the plague do not permit a clear understanding of the relationship between mortality and famine.

In England price increases, indicators of subsistence crises, are only moderately reflected by mortality.[32] The bad harvests of 1557, 1588 and 1597 had repercussions on the death-rate, amounting respectively to sixty, thirty and twenty-six per cent higher than the underlying trend. In the seventeenth century, the more localised food crisis of 1623 produced a relatively modest rise in mortality, while the sudden upsurge in prices in 1647–9 had only a moderate effect. In the second half of the seventeenth century, survival crises become rare. In the last decade of that century, a succession of years with very high prices and a consistent fall in real wages, the effect on mortality was minimal and, if anything, remained below the trend, in contrast to the rest of Europe. Crises in the eighteenth century are even rarer, particularly during the first decades of the century; and yet 1710 was a year of exceedingly high prices as a result of the poor harvest that followed the harsh European winter of 1709. 'Famine is not too hard a word to describe the conditions of that terrible year.'[33] The years

1727–30 and 1741–3, although characterised by mortality notably higher than normal, did not see large increases in prices. There is little similarity between the course of events in England and that in nearby Scotland or Holland, not to mention France.[34]

The French picture differs a great deal from the British one.[35] The seventeenth and eighteenth centuries, documented in great detail, testify amply to the tragic consequences of many subsistence crises, from the 1628–32 crisis (allied to the plague), to those at the 'Fronde' of 1649–54, to that of 1660–3, and to the devastating crises of 1693–4 and 1709–10. In every case there was an enormous rise in cereal prices: to two, three, even four times the normal levels, while the increase in deaths was by no means negligible either, doubling in comparison with adjacent years in 1693–4 and 1709–10. The end of Louis XIV's reign did not signal the end of the crises of the *ancien régime*: the high mortality due to the epidemic of 1740 was flanked by two years of poor harvest. Severe epidemic outbursts were interwoven with crises of subsistence, the latter not always preceding the former. A clearer and more complete picture would, of course, be obtained by distinguishing between the cereal-producing North, the Midi – perhaps richer in food resources – and Brittany, although the overall picture would remain largely unaltered.[36]

French chronology may be applied to a large part of central Europe. In Germany,[37] 1527–34 and 1570–1 stand out as years of subsistence crisis. In the following century, the Thirty Years War is one continuous story of devastation and famine. The crisis years of 1624–31 and 1648–51 had repercussions all over Europe, including Italy. With some difference in timing, Germany reflected France during its two great crises of 1693 and 1709. However, the economic-demographic *ancien régime* in Germany seems to end later, as the years 1740–1, 1771–4 and 1816–17 were memorable ones for hunger and mortality. Seventeenth-century German chronology coincides well with that of Sweden,[38] where the year 1773–4 was remembered as the year of hunger.

The picture in Italy was more varied, owing to greater climatic and cultural differences. The price series worked out by Parenti for Siena and Florence,[39] and a number of death series obtainable for Tuscany,[40] enable us to identify years of famine and to evaluate their demographic repercussions. Sudden peaks in grain prices (which doubled or tripled in comparison with previous normal years) occurred in 1529, 1540, 1549, 1555 and 1591. There was not, however, for each of these instances, a corresponding sudden increase in mortality in the various parts of Tuscany. In Figure 9, however, we can see the correspondence between price rise and a rise in mortality

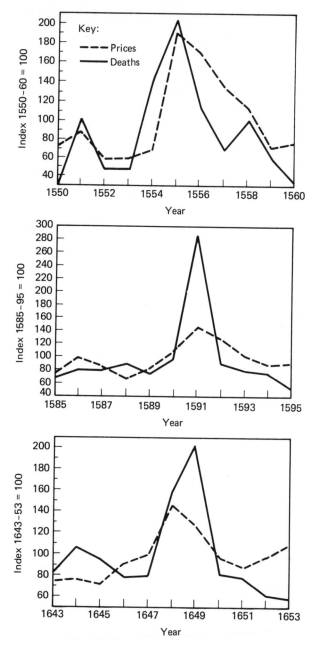

Figure 9 Indices for wheat prices and deaths in Siena, sixteenth to eighteenth centuries

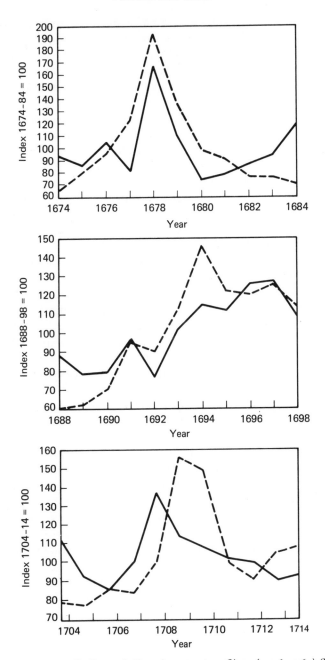

Sources: For prices: G. Parenti, *Prezzi e mercato a Siena (1546–1765)* (Florence, 1942), pp. 27–8; for deaths: unpublished series at the Statistics Department of the University of Florence.

around 1555, and again in 1591 – a particularly inauspicious year also for the area around Bologna.[41] In the following century, prices rocketed again in 1602, 1637, 1648, 1678 and 1694, as did mortality in 1602, in 1648 – a year of general European crisis – and in 1678. Increases in mortality were a good deal lower in 1637 and 1694. In the eighteenth century, the vulnerability to crises of subsistence seems less acute. The rise of prices in 1709–10, as in England, had little effect on mortality. On the other hand, the difficult years of 1764–7 had catastrophic consequences, especially in the South, and the same can be said of 1816–17, years of the last great European crisis.[42] It is almost always the case – and could not be otherwise – that a rise in mortality is brought on by epidemic attacks of quite identifiable diseases such as typhus. Figure 9, relating to Tuscany, illustrates the situation for some of these periods and attests to the weakening of the prices–mortality relationship from the sixteenth to the eighteenth centuries.

An empirical analysis of twelve historical series – for the most part relating to urban areas – of wheat prices and deaths from the end of the sixteenth century to the nineteenth century, has revealed that peaks (or troughs) in prices did not coincide completely with peaks (or troughs) in deaths. Out of 300 sub-periods examined, for about half (153) the relationship was direct, conforming to expectations; in a quarter of the cases (71) the relationship was inverse and contrary to expectations; while in the other quarter of the cases (76) there was no apparent relationship.[43]

For Spain, especially inland Spain, information is fairly abundant.[44] During the whole of the sixteenth century, the plague, endemic throughout, was the chief protagonist in the mortality crises, making it difficult to identify surges in mortality brought on by subsistence crises, with one clear exception at the beginning of the 1590s, which made itself felt elsewhere in Europe and preceded the terrible plague of 1594. In the seventeenth century, the years 1605–7, 1630–2, 1647–52, 1659–62 and 1680–4 were years of soaring prices and mortality crises, in many cases following the general European pattern. However, this century of economic decadence was notably less punctuated by mortality crises than the preceding 'siglo de oro'.[45] During the eighteenth century the crises of 1709 and 1764–7 were particularly conspicuous, and towards the end of the century agricultural and demographic crises were frequently associated. Nevertheless, the mortality crises that crowd the century are for the most part independent of subsistence crises.

Certain conclusions may be drawn within the limits of the thesis I have set out to illustrate:

1 From the sixteenth century and until the beginning of the nineteenth century, large increases in the price of grain, generally associated with limited food availability, gave rise to marked increases in mortality, even if there are several cases in which high prices found no appreciable correlation in mortality. This contradiction in economic impulses and demographic responses is well illustrated by Figure 10, relating to the 1709 crisis in England, northern France and Tuscany, when Europe was in the grip of an ice-cold winter. In the north of France, a doubling of wheat prices (on the Beauvais marketplace) in 1709 caused more than a doubling of the death-rate in the following year, but a similar peak in prices at Winchester had no effect on the English death-rate, which remained below the mean. In Tuscany, the peak in prices on the Siena market of 1709 was actually preceded, rather than followed, by a rise in the number of deaths.[46]

2 Surges in mortality were almost always caused directly – when it is possible to explore the documentation in depth – by outbreaks of clearly defined diseases such as typhus. In many cases the situation was complicated by overlaying factors such as the plague or war.

3 Surges in prices did not have uniform consequences: mortality was apparently less dependent on them in England than in the rest of Europe; less dependent in the French Midi than in the cereal-growing north of France; less dependent in areas of mixed cultivation or with a more extensive range of local resources than in areas with one predominant crop;[47] less dependent in the eighteenth century than in the seventeenth century. It is impossible to say whether these different reactions to the same price rise imply a differing reduction in food availability (due to varying degrees of home consumption, to food relief by local authorities, to the presence of substitute foodstuffs, to provisions in store, to varying income levels) or a different intensity of propagation of the epidemic circuit as a consequence of social dislocation brought on by a crisis of subsistence.

An econometric analysis of prices and mortality

The inferences emerging from qualitative examinations of the connections between subsistence crises and mortality have been recently considered in a number of econometric studies of England, France, Italy and Sweden. In particular, R. Lee has analysed series of wheat prices and deaths in England in order to establish the relationship between the annual deviations of these variables from the trend, and

to measure their association with each other.[48] The method used is
known as 'distributed lags', and makes it possible to measure the
effect of deviations in prices during a particular year (which we shall
call o) on a deviation in deaths in the same year (lag o) and in the
following years (lags 1, 2, 3 and 4). The assumption here is that the
negative effects of a famine would be felt not only in the number of
deaths occurring in the year affected by the shortage but also in
succeeding years. This is to some extent plausible: a famine may
create conditions favourable to the inception of an epidemic which

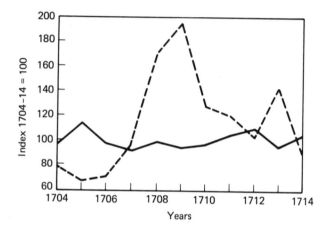

Key: — — — Prices in Winchester ———— Deaths in England

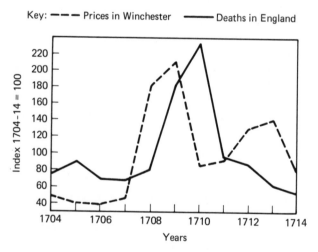

Key: — — — Prices in Oise ———— Deaths in Northern France

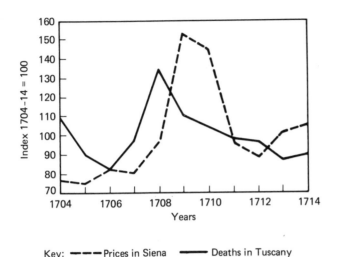

Key: ▬ ▬ ▬ Prices in Siena ▬▬▬ Deaths in Tuscany

Figure 10 Indices of wheat prices and deaths in England, France and Tuscany (1704–14 = 100)
Sources: Tuscany: for prices, G. Parenti, *Prezzi e mercato a Siena (1546–1765)* (Florence, 1942), pp. 27–8; for deaths, unpublished series at the Statistics Department of the University of Florence; England: for prices, Lord Beveridge, *Prices and Wages in England*, vol. I, *Price Table: Mercantile Era* (London, 1965), pp. 81–2; for deaths, E. A. Wrigley and R. S. Schofield, *The Population History of England, 1541–1871* (London, 1981), pp. 498–9; France: for prices, P. Goubert, *Beauvais et les Beauvaisis de 1600 à 1730* (Paris, 1920), pp. 404–5; for deaths, D. Rebaudo, 'Le mouvement annuel de la population française rurale de 1970 à 1740', *Population*, 24 (1979), no. 2, p. 596.

only develops after some time. Later, the population, having lost its burden of the less fit, will experience a 'rebound' in mortality which will decline to levels lower than normal. The hypothesis is, again, plausible, at least in theory. However, the span of time considered seems excessive, given that the consequences of an epidemic do not seem to extend beyond the year after its appearance, and it seems rather unrealistic to suppose that the 'rebound' effect could still be operating after three or four years.

Lee's results are interesting but contradictory. In the first place, while there does exist an association between fluctuations in price and fluctuations in mortality, the variance in the latter is explained only to a small extent by that of the former, being around 18% for the three centuries under discussion: 22% in 1548–1640; 17% in 1641–1745; 15% in 1746–1834. What is particularly surprising is that the 'sign' of the association is not consistent, as we can see from Table 9.

Table 9 *Coefficients of elasticity for deaths with respect to wheat prices in England, 1548–1834*

Delay	1548–1640	1641–1745	1746–1834	1548–1834
0	0.117	0.037	−0.016	0.048
1	0.155	0.073	0.020	0.090
2	0.165	0.098	−0.016	0.096
3	−0.008	−0.039	−0.038	−0.028
4	−0.082	−0.066	−0.083	−0.079
Total	0.347	0.103	−0.133	0.127
R^2	0.22	0.17	0.15	0.16

Source: R. D. Lee, 'Short-term Variations: Vital Rates, Prices and Weather' in Wrigley and Schofield, *The Population History of England, 1541–1871* (London, 1981), chapter 9.

This table gives the coefficients of elasticity of mortality with respect to a unit variation in prices. In other words, this coefficient measures the variations in deaths in the year of crisis and in the following years as that employed by Lee and relating to the period 1609–1760, has coefficients for each lag (from 0 to 4 years) are additive, and therefore the total coefficient represents the 'net' effect of variations on prices in a given year on the total deaths of the five year period.

According to Lee's result, a 100% increase in prices would have a 'net' effect on deaths of +34.7% for the period 1548–1640; +10.3% for 1641–1745; and −13.3% for 1746–1834. During the first two periods, an increase in prices causes an increase in deaths in years 0, 1 and 2 and a lagged reaction in years 3 and 4. This confirms the theoretical assumptions. However, in the third period the signs are negative for all lags except that of year 1, and the increase in prices actually brings about a 'net' reduction in the number of deaths over the period. The assumption is thus overturned.

Another interesting analysis has been carried out by Lee on the same series. Here he treats separately the reaction of mortality to increasingly large deviations from trend in prices,[49] that is, to whether the prices in the year under consideration were very low (−22% and below, compared to trend), low (−22% to 0), high (0 to +21%), very high (+21 to 44%) or extremely high (+44% and over). He finds that only in years with extremely high prices is there an appreciable effect on mortality. In fact, the net effect on deaths of 'very low prices' to 'very high prices' is either nil or equal to one or two percentage points, and so insignificant. Only 'extremely high' prices seem to have the effect of sending up the death-rate by fifteen per cent above trend. This analysis would seem to indicate, at least for England, the existence of a 'threshold' level in price variations below which the effect on the death-rate is virtually nil. Prices much lower than normal have no positive effect, however, on the death-rate.

Lee's results are not free from interpretative ambiguity. In the first place there is, over time, a progressive shift in the prices–mortality relationship, a fact which accords well with the hypothesis of a net nutritional improvement in the eighteenth and nineteenth centuries, as this improvement would reduce the sensitivity of a population's health to variations in purchasing power. The fact, moreover, that only very large price rises induce significant increments in the number of deaths can be interpreted in two different ways, not in themselves mutually exclusive:

1 The consumption of cereals is fairly rigid. Therefore only very marked increases in price cause a noticeable drop in consumption and a consequent increase in mortality.

2 Only when the drop in food availability is considerable is the deterioration in nutritional levels such as to provoke a rise in mortality.

The French case has been studied by Weir,[50] who compares it to that of England using the same method as Lee, but with a different periodisation because of the later start of the French death series (1670). His results are shown in Table 10. The period 1670–1739, characterised by the tragic crises of *ancien régime* France, conforms to expectations. The net coefficients are positive, and a 100% increase in prices provokes a 31% increase in deaths in England and one of 50% in France.[51] However, in the second period (1740–89) the correlation becomes negative, and even though the French crises after the reign of the Sun King had become 'disguised', to use Meuvret's successful definition, it is difficult to understand how a rise in prices could lead to a reduction in the death-rate, particularly in a country that in the second half of the eighteenth century suffered, like the rest of Europe, a net drop in real wages and where food supply was still limited.[52] The same may be said of England. In the final period, covering Revolution, Empire and Restoration, the coefficients for France, though somewhat confused, are again consonant with expectations, probably due to the dominant effect of the subsistence crisis of 1816–17, while in England the link between prices and mortality is virtually nil.

Another example of the relationship between prices and deaths –

Table 10 *Coefficients of elasticity for deaths with respect to wheat prices in England and France, 1670–1829*

Delay	1670–1739 England	1670–1739 France	1740–1789 England	1740–1789 France	1790–1829 England	1790–1829 France
0	0.010	0.452	−0.022	−0.180	0.058	0.141
1	0.185	0.177	−0.031	0.124	−0.125	−0.193
2	0.092	−0.025	−0.021	0.290	0.200	0.312
3	0.030	−0.072	−0.089	−0.442	−0.118	−0.022
4	−0.007	−0.030	−0.026	−0.244	−0.060	−0.048
Total	0.310	0.502	−0.189	−0.452	−0.045	0.190

Source: D. R. Weir, 'Life Under Pressure: France and England, 1670–1870', *Journal of Economic History*, 44 (1984), no. 1.

based, however, on a smaller number of events – relates to grain prices on the Sienese market, and deaths in Siena and a few other Tuscan localities (Arezzo, Montalcino, Anghiari, Rapolano) presumably dependent on the Sienese market. The analysis, of the same sort as that employed by Lee and relating to the period 1609–1760, has produced results which conform to expectations and which are similar to those obtained for England and France (see Table 11). To a 100% rise in prices there is a corresponding increase in deaths (cumulating lags over years 0 to 4) of 46% for the period 1609–69, 31% for the period 1670–1760 and 44% for the two periods taken together. The explained variance is relatively modest, and in all cases there is a negative rebound in years 2 and 4.[53]

The fact that prices and mortality in some periods bear a relationship contrary to that expected emphasises the importance of autonomous epidemic cycles independent of food availability. 'It was a period of truce for smallpox and fevers', exclaimed contemporary physicians attempting to explain the low English mortality of 1709–10 in spite of the disastrous harvest, and at the same time underlining the relative independence of the two phenomena.[54] The lower elasticity of deaths with respect to wheat prices in England has been explained as the concomitant of a better balanced and perhaps richer diet; of a greater choice of substitutes for wheat; of the fact, in short, that as far as the relationship between population and food resources was concerned, England enjoyed a regime of 'low pressure' when compared with the high pressure that oppressed the France of Louis XIV and his successors. The second part of the eighteenth century and the beginning of the nineteenth further 'released' the pressure,

Table 11 *Coefficients of elasticity for deaths in certain localities in Tuscany with respect to wheat prices in Siena, 1609–1760.*

Lag	1609–69	1670–1760	1609–1760
0	0.259	0.337	0.311
1	0.074	−0.027	0.076
2	−0.034	−0.009	−0.006
3	0.336	0.027	−0.121
4	−0.175	−0.022	−0.083
Total	0.460	0.306	0.439
R^2	0.12	0.20	0.13

Source: The data were kindly provided by Cristina Martelli who conducted a study into the links between prices and mortality in Tuscany at the University of Florence.

particularly in England, but also in France, Italy and Sweden.[55] This explanation, however, is far from obvious according to what can be gathered from other indices of the standard of living to be considered below.

However we look at the data, a fundamental problem remains that defies solution. What does a surge in the price of wheat (or other staple cereal) actually mean in relation to the availability of food and its consumption? What is the relationship between a variation in the quantity produced and offered on the market and a variation in price? Gregory King, at the end of the seventeenth century, advanced the hypothesis that between prices and quantity there existed a relationship of the following type: a 10% reduction in the quantities produced gave rise to a 30% increase in prices, a 20% reduction to an 80% increase and so on according to these pairs of values: −30 and +160%; −40 and +280%; −50 and +450%.[56] This came about, evidently, in cases where there was no possibility of substitution with alternative foodstuffs or of purchase on other markets. It accords, moreover, with the hypothesis of the rigidity of consumption of cereals as the staple European food. The complexity of the problem, however, is well illustrated by Parenti who, taking the period 1560–1666 in Siena based on the quantities of wheat harvested and its price, shows that to a reduction in harvest of 10%, 20%, 30% and 40%, there corresponded variations in price less than proportional and equal to 5%, 11%, 18% and 27% respectively.[57] Changes in the productive and distributive structure, in the quotas of produce set aside for home consumption and so on, can perhaps explain differences in the price–

quantity relationship and, therefore, in the relationship between price and mortality.[58]

According to the traditional demographic regime, which in some parts of Europe persisted even to the turn of this century, the great famines – three or four in each century – almost always had a perceptible effect on mortality. Their frequency then seems to diminish during the course of the eighteenth century. There is, however, no lack of strong price rises without corresponding repercussions on mortality, confirming the relative independence of epidemic cycles from productive cycles. Milder penury had no visible effect on mortality. This can be interpreted in two different ways: either that populations were living at a level comfortably above the malnutrition threshold so that a decrease in food consumption could be tolerated without causing harm,[59] or, alternatively, that populations have a strong capacity to adapt to nutritional stress and to tolerate considerable reductions in energy balance without serious threat to their survival. What is more, as we saw at the beginning of this chapter, individuals display a remarkable adaptability to calorie reduction, at least for short periods. This does not mean that famine had no consequences. It certainly did in the poorer and weaker sectors. It simply proves that the defensive mechanisms existed and did not remain inactive.

4

The starving and the well-fed

The élites and the masses: equal in the face of death?

History abounds with the most startling social contrasts. Among the most salient is that between the rich and poor man's table. The former was as varied for its meats, game, fish, spices, sweets and wine, as the latter was monotonous and poor, with bread as the undisputed staple, providing that this, too, was not scarce. An obvious approach, then, is to take advantage of that laboratory with which history provides us, and compare where possible the survival of those who fed on plentiful and varied fare with that of people whose fare was scanty, monotonous and irregular. This laboratory can also produce evidence supporting or refuting the theory that mortality is essentially dependent on nutrition because of the determining effect nutrition has on the efficiency of the body's immune system and by extension on its defences against infectious diseases and epidemics. If the theory is sound, those social groups who fed on a rich and varied diet should have enjoyed a lower mortality and greater life expectancy than the masses who lived in poverty and were, from time to time, the victims of serious shortages.

Even today, there are many obstacles to the study of differential mortality. Indeed, it seems impossible to carry out mutually comparable investigations of a similar nature for the past since this would require subdivision of the population by nutritional level, something which we know little about even for the present day. There is, however, a way of circumventing the difficulty. It seems highly likely, if not certain, that privileged groups like the aristocracy, the upper bourgeoisie, people in positions of authority – in other words the social élites, however defined – had ample and constant food resources. For example, it is estimated that at the Bishop of Arles' table, the members of his household enjoyed a daily fare correspond-

63

ing to 4,500 calories; the nuns of the Convent of Marcigny in Burgundy in 1640 consumed about 4,000 calories per day, while the students of the Collegio Borromeo at Pavia consumed between 4,000 and 5,000 calories during the years 1608–18.[1] And these are moderate rations when compared with the 6,000–7,000 daily calories of the Swedish court of King Erik in 1573, or the 7,000–8,000 daily calories of Cardinal Mazzarino's household in 1656–7.[2] Examples abound which demonstrate the free access to food enjoyed by the privileged classes. Nor was their fare threatened during times of shortage or poverty, since they were evidently fully able to call on ample reserves both of food and of money. If we add that, besides enjoying more and better food, the élites also had the advantage of notably better living conditions, allowing effective protection from foul weather, the avoidance of physical fatigue, and, if needed, an escape from contagion or other dangerous situations, then one is forced to conclude that they must have enjoyed a level of mortality notably lower than the rest of the population.

However, a quick examination of the available material on mortality among the upper classes places in serious doubt the assumption that the advantages conferred by wealth extended to a longer life expectancy. The best data we have are those for English peers,[3] whose life expectancy[4] is given in Figure 11, compared with estimates for the total population of England.[5] The results are really surprising. Between 1550 and 1750, the life expectancy for peers was roughly the same as that for the rest of the population (if anything, between 1575 and 1675, it tended to be lower): for peers it oscillated from a minimum of 32 years in 1650–75 to a maximum of 38.1 in 1725–50; for the rest of the population, from a minimum of 32 years in 1650–75 to a maximum of 38.0 in 1575–1600. It was during the course of the eighteenth century that peers finally gained the advantage by 1.1 year in the first quarter of the century, 4.3 in the second, and 9.1 in the third. But for almost two centuries, covering both the benign Elizabethan age and the catastrophic seventeenth century, parity was the norm. This situation of high mortality and minimal advantage for peers seems to date back to previous centuries, as shown by calculations which, while perhaps less exact, give a life expectancy of twenty-six years at age twenty for the generations born between 1350 and 1500. This represents a higher level of mortality than that for the least favoured of all the subsequent generations: the one born during the first quarter of the seventeenth century.[6] Nor, if we climb another rung of the social ladder, were the hopes of longevity any better among British ducal families: those born between 1330 and 1479 had a

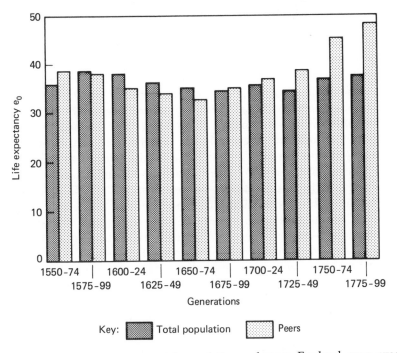

Figure 11 Life expectancy, e_0, total population and peers, England, 1550–1799
Sources: Life expectancy for peers: T. H. Hollingsworth, 'A Demographic Study of the British Ducal Families', *Population Studies*, 11 (1957), no. 1; for English population: E. A. Wrigley and R. S. Schofield, *The Population History of England, 1541–1871* (London, 1981), pp. 528–9.

life expectancy at birth of barely twenty-two years, which increases however to thirty-one years if deaths from violent causes are eliminated.[7] An analysis of English wills offers a similar picture, again for the upper classes: life expectancy at birth (calculated as an unweighted average for the two centuries before 1450) is around twenty-seven years, increasing to thirty if we remove the period 1346–1400 corresponding to the Black Death.[8] It is certain that in the late medieval era, after the mid-fourteenth century, the levelling effect of the plague effectively eliminated any advantage the upper classes may have had, always assuming this existed in the first place.

Although comparisons of this sort, between the privileged classes and the general population, are not possible for other populations, other indirect information tends to suggest that England was no exception. The reigning families of Europe, studied by Peller,[9] had a life expectancy of 34 years in the sixteenth century, of 30.9 in the seventeenth and 37.1 in the eighteenth. During the late Middle Ages (1100–1500) the levels were apparently somewhat lower.[10] Life expectancy for other national aristocracies, the Polish for example,[11] seem to follow this pattern. Among the old families of Geneva studied by Henry,[12] life expectancy at birth for both sexes was 28.5 years from 1550 to 1600, 32.1 during the first half of the seventeenth century and 35.0 during the second. Conditions improved noticeably only in the eighteenth century when mortality can at last be described as 'low' in terms of the traditional regime. Moreover, the clear drop in mortality in the eighteenth century seen in many of the selected groups is not independent of the contemporary and marked reduction in fertility due to the early spread of birth-control practices.[13] Also in Geneva, Perrenoud, who has studied the demography of the whole population of Geneva, finds great differences between social classes in the seventeenth century, differences which amount to a life expectancy for the rich almost double that of the poor. But he adds significantly, 'it is readily believed that social inequalities in mortality during the *ancien régime* were brought about by undernourishment and subsistence crises. This is not the case in Geneva, where from the sixteenth century there were no crises of this nature.'[14] In the city of Rouen, fluctuations in grain prices during the *ancien régime* had the same effect on mortality in the various social classes: a further proof of the weak dependence between mortality and social differences.[15]

For other selected groups we must content ourselves with estimates for mortality and life expectancy which exclude figures for childhood and adolescence, so that the overall death-rate is unknown. Nevertheless, it is significant that life expectancy calculated at age twenty is on the whole rather low and corresponds to values for life expectancy at birth of less than thirty years according to model life tables.[16] A few examples: for the dukes and peers of France, e_{20} 34.0;[17] for Jesuits entering the order between 1540 and 1565, 31.5,[18] the same value as that for the Danish nobility of the following century (31.6) and slightly higher than that for the Benedictines of Christ Church, Canterbury in the fifteenth century (30.6).[19] Among the Benedictines of Saint Maur, seventeenth-century longevity was markedly higher.[20] In other religious orders, for which admission was conditional on the novice's freedom from specific afflictions, the effect of selection should have reflected favourably on the lifespan, yet the facts do not bear this out.

The picture which emerges from these indications suggests that, at least in the sixteenth and seventeenth centuries, groups that were certainly privileged with regard to diet and the material aspects of life either had no advantages over the rest of the population (as in England), or suffered a very high level of mortality which is impossible to compare with that of the population as a whole. Both examples seem incompatible with the theory that nutrition was the dominant factor determining the mortality of the traditional regime. On the other hand, the marked diminution in the mortality among many groups in the eighteenth century is not easily explained by an improvement in food supplies since, already in the previous centuries, these seem to have been more than plentiful.

New countries and old countries

Entire populations, and not only the upper classes, stand out in the past as having had plentiful food resources, or at least more plentiful than those of other demographic groups. One might ask if these differences in food availability were reflected in any noticeable differences in mortality. I shall immediately add that the existence of a mortality differential is only to be expected if one espouses the theory that food is the single most prominent factor in the level of mortality. Anyone believing, or writing, that environmental and behavioural factors were far more influential must not expect decisive results from this study. An extreme example may serve to illustrate the limitations of this line of research. It is widely accepted that urban populations enjoyed better and more stable levels of nourishment than the rest of the population, due to the relative abundance of currency among city dwellers and the overall greater ability of governments to control supplies. It is not by chance that during famines the direction was from country to city and not the reverse. John Graunt, a keen and accurate observer, commented that in London 'few were starving' and that the 'vast number of *Beggars*, swarming up and down this City, do all live, and seem to be most of them healthy and strong'.[21] Yet the cities of the past were human conglomerations characterised by high mortality, higher than in the countryside. The factors of urban crowding, density and the transmissibility of infection were enough to counteract and override any advantage resulting from a richer, more varied and more stable diet.

Let us now look at larger aggregates: the 'new' countries of America, North and South, which during the nineteenth century attracted so many millions of immigrants driven, if not by hunger – like the Irish after the Great Famine of 1845 – at least by great economic hardship, including poor nourishment, which afflicted rural areas all over Europe. The new countries did not suffer from famines except in rare cases, and dietary well-being was undoubtedly wide-spread. Diets were reasonably good in America because land was accessible. There is no record, except for the earliest years, of famines similar to those that hit part of Europe in the late seventeenth century. When food had to be imported as a result of temporary short-ages, good water transportation and frequent surpluses in neighbouring colonies made it readily available.[22] Settling along the St Lawrence River, the first French colonisers of Canada (the gener-ations of 1650–1720) had a life expectancy at birth of 35.5 years, a level presumably higher than that in contemporary France, but not very different from England.[23] By the middle of the last century a newborn in the United States could count on a life expectancy between thirty-seven and forty-three years[24] – a level equalling the average for the countries from which the American population had originated, despite the poverty of the peasant masses on the old continent keen to cross the ocean to improve their lot. In Argentina, where the diet was certainly not deficient in animal proteins – Darwin observed that 'the gaucho touches nothing but meat for months on end'[25] – mortality was still quite high in the second half of the nineteenth century. Life expectancy at birth for the whole population has been estimated at 32.5 years of age in Buenos Aires in 1855, at 25.4 years in 1868–70 (there being an epidemic of cholera) and 31.7 in 1887. Only at the end of the century did it reach forty years. The picture is com-pleted by estimates for the whole of Argentina:[26] life expectancy at birth for the last third of the century (1869–95) was thirty- three years, roughly the same as that for Italy in a period when the northern peasantry was dying of pellagra and the rural populations ate meat only on certain feast-days. In Brazil, further north, the life expectancy in Parana around 1822 was just short of twenty-nine years, a rather modest level.[27] Even at the end of the century, countries like Costa Rica and Chile had extremely low life expectancies of thirty years or less.[28]

Theory suggests that the low density of population in America and the slower rate of urban agglomeration, as well as the greater avail-ability of food supplies, should have led to a greater resistance to infection on the part of the population and therefore greater longevity. But the data do not corroborate this hypothesis. It would certainly be interesting to know more about the first settlements in New Zealand or Australia, where diets must have been similar, if not better, than those in America.

Three points seem to emerge from this examination of life expec-tancy among the upper classes and in the New World:

1 Differential mortality in the past – if we take the assumed levels of food intake as the determining variable – seem to be modest, in fact barely visible, at least in some cases (English peers for instance).

2 The mortality of the upper classes, who presumably never had a serious problem of food availability, was fairly high and declined significantly only in the eighteenth and nineteenth centuries, thereby widening the gap with the rest of the population. This is not unlike the case of fertility which seems to respond more to social and cultural factors than to biological or nutritional ones.

3 In spite of their undoubted dietary superiority, American populations seem to have had, in the last century, a mortality experience similar to that of European populations.

The evidence we have accumulated is certainly not decisive. Differences in mortality have their roots in a plurality of causes, including nutrition. It would be foolish to deny that nutrition had an effect on the degree of mortality. To maintain that it had a decisive effect, however, would seem unfounded, as the new data we have discussed demonstrate.

An interlude: changes in mortality transition in the eighteenth century

In the course of time there have been profound cyclical changes in mortality levels, as shown in the first chapter. The late medieval cycle is well documented, as are the seventeenth-century decline and the improvement of the eighteenth century. Prior to the end of the eighteenth century, though, we lack accurate estimates of mortality for large aggregates which would enable us to observe the 'structure' of changes in the mortality levels by age, sex, cause of death and so on and consequently to better discuss the possible causes of fundamental variations. Beginning with the eighteenth century, our knowledge becomes broader, at least for some countries, and deeper induction can be attempted.

From Table 12 we can deduce a net decrease in mortality in four European countries between the late eighteenth and the middle of the nineteenth centuries. It is difficult to say whether analogous decreases took place in other parts of Europe, for instance in Germany, Italy and Spain, where information is more fragmentary. But to judge from the high levels still prevalent in the middle of the nineteenth century, improvements in survival rates – which did occur in certain cases – must have been relatively modest.[29] It should also be noted that in traditional demographic regimes, the higher the level of mortality the greater the influence (on the overall level of mortality) of

Table 12 *Life expectancy at birth for some European populations in the eighteenth and nineteenth centuries*

Period	England	France	Sweden	Denmark
1700–9	36.8	—	—	—
1710–19	36.5	—	—	—
1720–9	32.5	—	—	—
1730–9	31.8	—	—	—
1740–9	33.5	24.8	—	—
1750–9	36.9	27.9	37.3	—
1760–9	34.6	27.7	36.3	—
1770–9	36.9	28.9	34.0	—
1780–9	35.3	27.8	35.8	34.9
1790–9	37.0	31.1	39.1	40.4
1800–9	37.3	33.9	36.5	41.8
1810–19	37.7	36.5	39.1	42.2
1820–9	39.6	38.8	42.8	40.9
1830–9	40.5	38.1	42.7	37.4
1840–9	39.9	39.9	45.0	44.1
1850–9	40.0	39.8	43.3	—

Sources: England: E. A. Wrigley and R. S. Schofield, *The Population History of England*, table A3.1; France: Y. Blayo, 'La mortalité en France de 1740 à 1829' in *Population*, 30 (1975), special number; Sweden, based on data from *Historisk Statistik för Sverige*, Stockholm, 1969; Denmark: O. Andersen, 'The Decline of Danish Mortality before 1850 and its Economic and Social Background' in *Pre-Industrial Population Change*, ed. G. Fridlizius *et al.*

deaths resulting from infectious diseases, so that a reduction in mortality must follow a reduction of the latter. Unfortunately, reliable statistics on cause of death are available only from the second half of the nineteenth century, too recent an era for them to be useful in the present context. However, for the purposes of illustration and for three countries with 'precocious' statistics on the causes of death, Table 13 shows the influence of various types of infectious diseases on overall mortality. Clearly the influence of this group of diseases on mortality was greatest in Italy (fifty-six per cent) where life expectancy was thirty-three years, and lowest in New Zealand (forty per cent) which enjoyed a life expectancy more than twenty years greater at the same date (1881). Furthermore, the incidence of infectious diseases is considerably higher in infancy and tends to decrease with advancing age.

Consequently the first transition from high to not so high mortality, concurring with the passage from the eighteenth to the nineteenth century, must have entailed: (a) quite a large reduction in mortality

Table 13 *Incidence of certain groups of infectious disease on mortality in some countries in the nineteenth century*

Cause of death	Italy 1881	England 1861	New Zealand 1881
Respiratory, TB	6.5	11.5	7.7
Other infectious and parasitical	24.1	15.0	14.3
Influenza, pneumonia, bronchitis	14.1	12.7	10.1
Diarrhoea	11.6	5.9	7.8
Total specified infections	56.3	45.1	39.9
Other causes	43.7	54.9	60.1
Total deaths	100	100	100
Life expectancy (e_o)	33.6	41.8	55.0

Source: S. H. Preston, N. Keyfitz and R. Schoen, *Causes of Death: Life Tables for National Populations* (New York, 1972).

(more than proportional with respect to other causes of death) due to infectious causes; and (b) a substantially larger reduction, relatively speaking, in infant and child mortality as compared to that of the middle-aged or elderly. Indeed, it can be said that the extension of the average lifespan came about chiefly due to a drop in the extremely high level of mortality up to the age of ten.

Point (a) cannot be fully demonstrated because of the lack of stable data on causes of death, although supportive indications are many.[30] Point (b) is a necessary sequel to point (a) and is amply demonstrated in a number of populations. Figure 12 shows the variations in the probability of death for certain age groups in the eighteenth and nineteenth centuries in several European countries. The pattern of these variations conform as a rule, though with many exceptions, to expectations. It will be noticed in passing that absolute variations in the risk of death are greater in the first year of life (which also has the highest death-rate)[31] and diminish with increasing age.

I shall not enter here into the thorny though important debate concerning the evaluation of individual factors in the decline of mortality during the eighteenth century. Nutrition, hygiene, medicine, the virulence of infection, and immunological resistance all play a part, but it is difficult to determine the extent of their contributions or their mutual interactions. On the other hand, the evolution of each of the factors in a direction favourable to survival would, by and large, have had a greater effect on the younger age-groups than on the older ones, as shown in Figure 12. Medicine at that time undoubt-

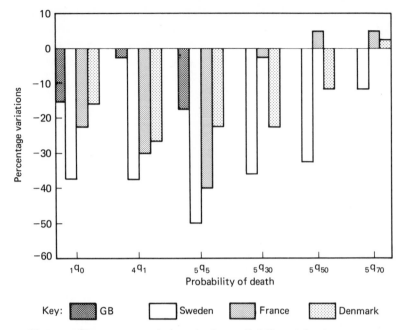

Figure 12 Percentage variations in the probability of death in certain countries during the first mortality transition, eighteenth to nineteenth centuries.
Note: England: percentage variation between 1700–49 and 1750–99; France: 1740–49 and 1820–29; Sweden: 1760–69 and 1820; Denmark: 1780–89 and 1820–29.

edly contributed to reducing the incidence of smallpox, highest between the ages of one and five: hygiene, by lowering the rate of transmission of pathogenic agents, may have reduced the incidence of a number of infectious diseases, especially among children and younger people; nutrition, by strengthening the body's immune defences, may have benefited all ages most vulnerable to infectious processes. In short, a purely 'demographic' examination of mortality trends tells us little about individual causes. There are a few exceptions, however, one of which we shall examine in the following section.

Nutrition and infant mortality

At the beginning of this chapter I mentioned the nutritional disparities between social classes and, to some extent, between whole populations. But there is a phase in life, corresponding more or less with the first year, during which types of nutrition in past times must have been fairly uniform. These bore no affinity to the varying food availability which, as we have seen, was an important factor in the temporary fluctuations of whole populations. During all or most of the first year of life, babies were fed on mother's milk, a complete nourishment in itself which above all provided the child with essential immunological defences against infection. It is true that there were significant exceptions to the universal practice of breast-feeding; we need only recall the various forms of wet-nursing, or the very early weaning practised in some, albeit limited, areas,[32] or the fate of babies who lost their mother or were put in the care of charitable institutions.[33] However, even taking into account the many notable exceptions, there is no doubt that maternal breast-feeding was the most usual form of feeding in the first year of life, and so this age group was almost entirely exempt from the nutritional vicissitudes to which older groups were exposed. If this statement is correct (and we shall dwell on it further in the following section) and if the nutritional factor was foremost in determining human survival, it follows that the levels of infant mortality in the past should show a conspicuous uniformity, or at least a lesser differentiation than that for other ages of childhood.

Anyone familiar with the results of historical demography is well aware that, at the local level, the variability in figures for infant mortality was strikingly high. But given the frequent failure to register the deaths of new-born babies in the past and the vigorous process of corrections and estimates necessary to fill the gaps in the basic material, local studies are not altogether trustworthy. Let us take, therefore, certain national groups and their infant and child mortality figures as shown in Table 14, which refers to the second half of the eighteenth century. True, we are dealing with the tail-end of *ancien régime* mortality, which was already declining as the nineteenth century drew closer, but we do not believe that this weakens the validity of our examination. Indeed, we see how variable infant mortality actually was: the probability of death before the first birthday varies between 165 per thousand in England and 273 in France, with Sweden and Denmark taking intermediate positions. It will be noted that the difference between infant mortality alone in France and in England corresponds (assuming identical mortality after the first year of life) to about four years of life expectancy at birth.[34] The same table also shows considerable differences in death-rates for later ages up to age fifteen. However, if the nutritional factor were decisive in determining disparities in mortality between ages one and four, or five and nine, it would be difficult to understand the existence of equally great differences in the first year of life. These observations

Population and nutrition

Table 14 *Infant and child mortality in four European countries during the second half of the eighteenth century*

Probability of death ($1000q_x$)	France (1750–99)	England (1750–99)	Sweden (1750–90)	Denmark (1780–1800)
${}_1q_0$	273	165	200	191
${}_4q_1$	215	104	155	156
${}_5q_5$	91	33	63	42
${}_5q_{10}$	42	21	34	—
l_{15}	491	736	612	641

Sources: France: Y. Blayo, 'La mortalité en France de 1740 à 1829', *Population*, 30 (1975), special number, pp. 138–9; England: E. A. Wrigley and R. S. Schofield, 'English Population History from Family Reconstitution: Summary Results', *Population Studies*, 37 (1983), no. 2, p. 177; Sweden: *Historisk Statistik för Sverige* (Stockholm, 1969); Denmark: O. Andersen, 'The Decline in Danish Mortality Before 1850 and its Economic and Social Background' in G. Fridlizius *et al.* (eds.), *Pre-Industrial Population Change* (Stockholm, Almquist and Wiksell, 1984).

regarding variations between populations in a given period also apply to the variations over time, which up to age fifteen are very similar, recorded in Figure 12.[35]

If we now descend to subnational levels – without embarking on studies of extreme cases and limiting ourselves to a few fairly broad regions of reliable data – we find that the variability mentioned in a national context is confirmed. We can take as an example the French regions in the sample by INED[36] for the period 1750–79, where infant mortality (q_0) ranged from a minimum of 191 per thousand in the south-west to a maximum of 292 per thousand in the north-east; or the villages and country towns of England in the eighteenth century, where it ranged from under 100 per thousand in Devon villages to 200 to 300 per thousand in towns like Banbury and Gainsborough.[37] We can pick out, too, from the now extensive literature available, a study of fifty-one Finnish parishes in the second half of the eighteenth century where three had a very low infant mortality (less than 100 per thousand) and two a very high one (over 300 per thousand), the intermediate distribution being very dispersed. Striking variations can also be found in Sweden,[38] Belgium,[39] Italy,[40] and in most other populations adequately studied.

We can therefore conclude that, under the traditional demographic regime, differences in death-rates during the first year of life could easily reach 200 points per thousand which, given the observed death-rates for older ages, correspond roughly to seven or eight years of life expectancy.[41] These differences were presumably independent of the nutritional factors which for later ages were regarded as being so influential on mortality.

Factors relating to infant mortality in the 'ancien régime'

At the risk of straying somewhat from our central theme – the relationship between sustenance and mortality – it would be useful to go deeper into the mechanisms of mortality during the most vulnerable year of life, that between birth and the first birthday. Taking the first birthday as the terminal in studies of infant mortality is in fact an arbitrary convention. One ought, instead, to take the whole (variable) period from birth until weaning, when the transition to an 'external' form of nutrition is completed, with all the adaptations that such a delicate phase involves. However, what interests us here, and complements the themes of the last two sections, is to discuss the factors of first-year mortality – which as we have seen varied substantially with time and place – and consider the extent to which it might be independent of the purely nutritional factor.[42] More particularly, we must look at the effect of maternal breast-feeding, of its beginning, duration and end, of various weaning methods, and of other environmental and social factors.

It is likely that a baby's health and survival depend in part upon its mother's health and nutritional condition. It is through this mechanism that the nutritional level of the community can affect the chances of survival of the baby. A woman who is breast-feeding has a greater energy requirement than one who is not. Undernourishment reduces the volume of milk and probably also the fat and vitamin content in the milk. Nevertheless, the process of breast-feeding seems to be remarkably adaptable, in the sense that it permits, at least partially, the insulation of the baby from any nutritional stress suffered by the mother. Indeed, apart from cases of extreme malnutrition, women who are inadequately nourished are still able to breast-feed their babies quite normally, nor does the mother's undernourishment seem to affect the duration of the breast-feeding period. Significant in this context are the results of a comparative study of undernourished Indian women (1,200–1,600 calories per day), some breast-feeding, others not. After twelve months the latter weighed scarcely two kilos less than the former. 'This suggests that some process of metabolic adaptation, possibly due to higher prolactin levels, occurs in lactating women, allowing energy balance to be maintained on what would appear to be an inadequate diet.'[43] A state of undernourishment, especially in marginal sectors or in years of scarcity and famine, certainly has a negative effect on mothers, as on the rest of the population, but the maternal relationship reduces this negative effect both on the foetus during pregnancy and on the baby during breast-feeding.

Alternatively, the influence of breast-feeding – until weaning and beyond – on infant survival is considerable. A baby's immunological defences at birth are very weak and maternal breast-feeding provides immunological protection, a point scientifically well-established. Unlike other baby foods, both colostrum and maternal milk contain biologically active substances that protect the infant from infection: 'The concentration of these substances is higher in the colostrum, the high protein fluid secreted in the first days postpartum when the infant's immune system is still immature.'[44]

Breast-feeding does not begin in all cultures at the same time. Some scholars believe that, following the teachings of Soranus, it became the practice in the late Middle Ages to delay breast-feeding by a day or two, so that the child should avoid being administered colostrum, thought harmful.[45] This custom is echoed in sixteenth-century treatises: 'Thus indeed milk in this period is indigestible, heavy and corrupt, on which account the Latins call it colostrum.'[46] Substitutes are recommended in the form of artificial paps and even mild purgatives to stimulate the expulsion of the meconium and give the mother time to form her milk. Two centuries later, in the eighteenth century, doctors and paediatricians preached a different gospel: not only was it understood that there was no real substitute for a mother's milk, but women were also exhorted to start breast-feeding immediately, as the nutritive and protective qualities of colostrum became finally recognised.[47] An extensive analysis of published medical literature on the subject has shown that in Great Britain before 1673 'all writers condemned colostrum as harmful or undesirable', while after 1748 'no writer considered colostrum was a bad or harmful substance'.[48] This is not to say that people conformed with medical opinion. At best, medical opinion represents a 'learned' pointer to a change of attitude.[49] However, more than one author has maintained that effective changes in breast-feeding practices did take place and had an important influence on mortality during the first month of life. In Great Britain, 'changes towards early maternal breast-feeding during the eighteenth century contributed to a notable decline in mortality (nought to twenty-eight days) and a decrease in maternal morbidity and mortality from milk fever'.[50]

But independent of the earlier or later start of breast-feeding, its duration, and therefore the age at weaning, play a primary role in infant survival, as so many studies both historical and contemporary have demonstrated beyond any doubt. Babies who have not been breast-fed possess a defective immunological system and are prone to catch gastro-intestinal and viral respiratory infections. They run a far greater risk of death than breast-fed infants, a fact amply demonstrated by the tragic fate of babies in orphanages and by the very high mortality in those rare areas where breast-feeding was discredited. The protective effect of breast-feeding lasts, by and large, for the whole of the first year and thereafter decreases due to diminished flow. The age of weaning is thus an important variable in infant survival. If weaning occurs too early the infant is liable to catch infections, a risk which increases (whatever the weaning age may have been) at the point when the infant starts to take food that is handled and therefore easily contaminated.[51]

Eighteenth-century treatises are all in favour of maternal breast-feeding, and not a few authors associate an improvement in infant mortality at the end of that century with both the immediate start of breast-feeding and also its prolongation, particularly in areas where early weaning had prevailed.[52] Unfortunately there are no quantitative data on the duration of breast-feeding and on ages at weaning. Thus any conclusions drawn about their influence on infant mortality must be largely inductive. Nonetheless it is probable that changes in custom relevant to first year mortality were mainly those occurring in the first six months of life: in the traditional mortality regime a good half of infant deaths occurred in the first month of life, and between seventy and ninety per cent in the first six months.[53] Since patterns of breast-feeding, apart from the moment of its inception, could not have varied that much during the first few months of life, we must look for other factors to explain variations in mortality.

These often crucially important factors have to do with environmental circumstances, climate, method of upbringing and greater or lesser vigilance in caring for the child. There is a great deal of evidence that these factors were predominant in determining the levels of infant mortality (with the exception of those groups and areas where breast-feeding was looked upon with disfavour). It would not otherwise be possible to explain the enormous infant mortality differences between winter and summer births, recorded in some areas but not in others with identical climatic patterns.[54] How the child was protected from the cold was tremendously important. In some areas this was done efficiently, in others very poorly. High infant mortality in some areas can be explained by the employment of mothers outside the home and so by more relaxed supervision of the child.[55] Finally, the wide divergence in infant mortality in urban areas between different social strata was attributable above all to environmental factors, such as the density of living conditions and the easier transmission of infections.[56]

Let us retrace our path through the previous sections and emphasise several points:

1 In the first 'modern' mortality transition, which took place between the eighteenth and nineteenth centuries in a number of European countries, there was substantial mortality decline among infants and children, and a lesser reduction for older age groups. The probable explanation is that mortality was checked as a result of better control of the causes of death linked to infectious diseases, the incidence of which decreases with increasing age. However, there are no notable differences between variations in the first year of life and those in later childhood. This may be surprising, since the risks of death in the first year depend mostly on breast-feeding practices, whereas those in later years depend, according to the nutritional hypothesis, on general nutritional levels, which would presumably have improved over the period.

2 We have also observed that in the traditional demographic regime, variations in infant mortality between one population and another, or between one period and another, could by themselves cause variations in life expectancy equal to three to four years for each 100 point variation in mortality (expressed as rates per thousand). Thus infant mortality alone could be a primary cause of variations in the total mortality.

3 Point 2 leads one to seek an explanation for the great variability in infant mortality. We noted that the influence of the nutritional state of the mother was slight, whereas the moment of inception of breast-feeding and the method and age of weaning, where premature, could exercise a strong influence. Since, however, over three-quarters of first-year mortality was concentrated in the first six months, and since weaning rarely occurred before that age, it can be inferred that the source of variation must be put down to environmental, climatic and cultural factors inherent in the baby's upbringing.

4 We can also conclude that in the years succeeding the first, the factors listed at the end of point 3 would be of more than just secondary importance, and would perhaps be predominant in comparison with purely nutritional factors.

5

Food and standard of living: hypotheses and controversies

Soundings in a vast sea

Up to this point we have dealt with various controversial aspects of the relationship between nutrition, health and mortality. It is time now to address a question which has thus far remained in the background: What can we say about long-term dietary trends in European societies? Did these historical populations fight a ceaseless battle against the scarcity of resources; or did they on the whole live well above the threshold of malnutrition; or might they have fluctuated over long periods between comfortable plenty and dire hardship? And supposing these trends can be ascertained, how do they fit in with mortality trends?

It is important to state at the outset that a satisfactory account of Europe's nutritional history does not exist.[1] Agricultural history, though abounding in comprehensive studies on cultivation techniques and yield, land management and price trends, is very uninformative when it comes to the estimation of production flows which would enable estimation of consumption levels. Nevertheless, a few soundings have been made which enable the measurement of long-term changes in nutritional patterns and it is to these that we shall refer in this chapter. These soundings take the form of estimates of food budgets in a number of communities and their assumed caloric content; levels of consumption for some staples like bread or meat; the spread and contribution to diets of new crops such as maize and potatoes; comparisons of wage and price trends for the main food-stuffs (mainly cereals) as indicators of the purchasing power and the standard of living of certain classes of the population; and variations in stature as a 'net' indicator of the community's level of nutrition. From this range of indicators we cannot expect to get an unequivocal and absolute response regarding the relationship between mortality

79

trends and changes in nutritional level, but at least it provides the basis for a logical set of references and a series of interpretive assumptions corroborated by a few proofs. The principal series of soundings consists of estimates of food consumption in certain populations. These estimates are usually as bold as they are uncertain, an observation reinforced by the fact that even today, rather than face the difficult task of making consumption surveys, the general preference is for anthropometric studies in which the results, measured against pre-determined standards, provide only indirect information about levels of nutrition.[2]

Let us return to estimates of food budgets and caloric balance which can be derived both from studies of family or institutional consumption based on purchase-lists and account ledgers, and from aggregate studies based on the relationship between food supply (in theory production for consumption, net of changes in stocks and the balance of trade) and population. Both these methods are beset by many problems which multiply the further back one goes in time due to the poor quality and quantity of available information. We can only note the difficulty of calculating the consumption of home-produced goods, typically substantial and varied in predominantly farming communities; the uncertain quantity of food decayed, discarded and wasted; the accumulation or running down of stocks, whether of the family or the community. If, having determined the quantities available for consumption, one then wishes to calculate their caloric content, other problems arise, due to the difficulty of assigning correct conversion coefficients to food whose quality is unknown, or because changes are brought about in the nutritional value of food by its mode of preparation, and also because of the uncertain nutritional value of wines and beers. Finally, once we have established the average levels of consumption and caloric intake for a given community, there remains the question of inequalities: the more unequal the access to food by different sections of a community, the less useful our average figures will be.[3]

A number of studies do exist which attempt to reconstruct food and caloric balances for populations at different times in the past. We shall exclude the caloric estimates for certain special cases (such as royal households or the households of the higher nobility and clergy) which, though useful if one wishes to reconstruct the life styles, diet and consumption patterns of the privileged, are hardly to our purpose here. These include the examples of King Erik's court in the sixteenth century – with an average daily caloric consumption per head of 6,500 – of Mazzarino's household in the seventeenth century which averaged 7,000 calories per head, and of Duke Magnus whose court consumed even more.[4] The estimates are mind-boggling and certainly gout-inducing, though it is some consolation to know that behind such apparent waste, a far from meagre stream of surplus food made its way onto the tables of servants' and stable-attendants' families, ready to satisfy their robust appetites.

Also of limited interest are budgets and estimates relating to particular communities, whether military (especially the rations of naval crews and civil and religious colleges and monasteries) or the objects of charity or incarceration (hospitals, hospices and prisons). Although these communities often kept reliable accounts (but how can we be sure that all purchases benefited only those on whose behalf they were ostensibly made?), they can hardly be deemed representative of the population as a whole. Certainly the 5,000 daily calories of a student at the Collegio Borromeo at Pavia in the seventeenth century cannot have been within the reach of the average city dweller with his cereal-based diet.[5] The sick at the hospital of Caen could count on up to 3,000 calories a day, but this was probably because their condition required a higher than average supply of energy. If soldiers and sailors, whether Venetian or Tuscan, Swedish or Russian, French or English, received rations generally in excess of 3,000 or 4,000 calories per day[6] to equip them with the energy required for the exercise of their martial or navigational arts, this does not mean that the civil population enjoyed the same diet, though some maintain this was the norm rather than the exception.[7]

If we pass from the investigations of such communities, certainly privileged as far as food was concerned, to studies of large, or at any rate larger, groups of 'ordinary' people, we should examine the results carefully because of their possible demographic importance. In Table 15 and Figure 13 I have summarised a few scattered data, drawn from all over Europe from the fourteenth to the twentieth century, relating to the caloric intake of various populations. The reliability of all the sources used here, whether remote or recent, is uncertain and so of course is the data derived: the real nutritional value of the various foodstuffs involved, the estimates of reductions in consumption, waste, and above all the amounts contributed by home-produce. These results, in so far as they represent soundings of a submerged and largely unknown world, suggest caloric levels generally higher than, and indeed in some cases even double, the 2,000 daily per capita calories I have suggested as adequate for an *ancien régime* population. The only case that falls below this mark is that of France in 1780–90 and 1803–12 as given in Toutain's estimates.[8]

Table 15 *Caloric balance of some European populations, fourteenth to twentieth centuries (daily calories per head)*

No.	Place	Period	Categories observed	Daily calories per head
1	Sweden	1550	Royal serfs	4,200
2	Sweden	1600s	Royal serfs	3,523
3	Sweden	1700s	Royal serfs	3,980
4	Sweden	1730–1820	Iron workers	3,000–3,900
5	England (Hunstanton, Norfolk)	1342	Farmhands (harvest)	5,368
6	England (Sedgeford, Norfolk)	1424	Farmhands	5,735
7	England	1400s	Peasants	3,200
8	England	1400s	Meat-eating class	4,750
9	England	1826	Population	2,050
10	Poland (Nowe Miasto)	1560–70	Royal serfs	4,427
11	Poland	1500s	Farmhands	3,500
12	Germany (Saxony)	1500s	Farmhands	3,446
13	Low Countries (Anvers)	1596–1600	Labourers	2,240
14	Belgium	Late 1700s	Population	2,510
15	Belgium (Ghent)	Early 1800s	Population	2,435
16	France (Languedoc)	1480	Farmhands	4,163
17	France (Languedoc)	1580–90	Farmhands	4,917
18	France (Toulouse)	1600s–1700s	Population	2,840
19	France (Gevaudan)	1754–67	Peasants	1,740–2,000
20	France (Paris)	1780	Population	1,950–2,350
21	France	1781–90	Population	1,753–2,130
22	France	1803–12	Population	1,846
23	France	1845–54	Population	2,480
24	France	1885–94	Population	3,220
25	Italy (Sicily)	1688–1705	Farmhands	2,900–3,450
26	Italy (Sicily)	1681–6	Urban population	3,480

27	Italy	1861–80	Population	2,637
28	Italy	1880–1900	Population	2,158
29	Italy	1937–9	Population	2,702
30	Italy (North)	1937–9	Population	2,539
31	Italy (Central)	1937–9	Population	2,285
32	Italy (South)	1937–9	Population	2,631
33	Italy (Islands)	1937–9	Population	2,539

Sources: Sweden: M. Essemyr and M. Morell, 'Changes in Swedish Nutrition since the Seventeenth Century', *Ninth Economic History Congress* (Bern, 1986). The estimates given by the two authors are revised with data from E. Heckscher, *An Economic History of Sweden* (Cambridge, Mass.: Harvard University Press, 1954), pp. 69, 116, 149; England (Hunstanton and Sedgeford, Norfolk): C. Dyer, 'Changes in Nutrition and Standard of Living in England, 1200–1550', *Ninth Economic History Congress* (Bern, 1986); England: H. Neveux, 'L'alimentation du XIVème au XVIIIème siècle', *Revue d'Histoire Economique et Sociale*, 51 (1973), no. 3, p. 376. The data are drawn from J. C. Drummond and A. Wilbraham, *The Englishman's Food, A History of Five Centuries of English Diet*, revised ed. D. Hollingsworth (London, 1957), p. 467; Poland (Nowe Miasto): A. Wyczanski. 'La consommation alimentaire en Pologne au XVIème siècle', *Pour une Histoire de l'Alimentation*, J. J. Hémardinquer (ed.), *Cahiers des Annales*, 28 (1970), 46; Poland and Germany (Saxony): A. Wyczanski and M. Dembinska, 'La nourriture en Europe Centrale au début de l'Age Moderne', *Ninth Economic History Congress* (Bern, 1986); Low Countries (Anvers): W. Abel, *Congiuntura agraria e crisi agraria* (Turin, Einaudi, 1976), p. 211; Belgium: P. Scholliers, 'Roles of Production, Social Policy and Nutrition in Belgium in the Nineteenth and Twentieth Centuries', *Ninth Economic History Congress* (Bern, 1986); Belgium (Ghent): C. Vandenbroeke, 'L'alimentation à Gand pendant la première moitié du XIXème siècle', *Annales ESC*, 30 (1975), nos. 2–3, p. 589; France (Languedoc): E. Le Roy Ladurie, *Les Paysans de Languedoc* (Paris, 1966), vol. I, p. 267; France (Toulouse): B. Benassar and J. Goy, 'Contribution à l'histoire de la consommation alimentaire du XIVème au XIXème siècle', *Annales ESC*, 30 (1975). nos. 2–3, p. 414; France (Gevaudan and Paris): H. Neveux, 'L'alimentatation', p. 376; France: J.-C. Toutain, 'La consommation alimentaire en France de 1789 à 1964', *Economies et Sociétés*, Cahiers de l'ISEA, vol. A, no. 11 (Geneva, 1971), p. 1977. The highest estimate for 1781–90 was calculated on the basis, not used by the author, of the 'high' series of cereal consumption; Italy (Sicily): M. Aymard and H. Bresc, 'Nourritures et consommation en Sicile entre XIVème et XVIIIème siècles', *Annales ESC*, 30 (1975), nos. 2–3, pp. 587–8; Italy (1861–1900): ISTAT, *Statistiche storiche dell'Italia 1861–1900* (Rome, 1976), p. 159; Italy (1937–9): S. Somogyi, 'L'alimentazione nell'Italia unita', *Storia d'Italia*, vol. V: *I documenti* (Turin, 1973), p. 864. The data are drawn from the study by G. Galeotti and L. Livi and given by G. Galeotti in *Geografia regionale dei consumi alimentari', Atti del convegno di studi sull'orientamento dei consumi alimentari* (Rome, 1964).

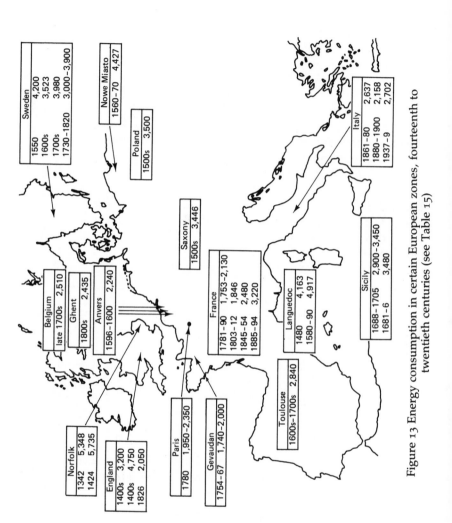

Figure 13 Energy consumption in certain European zones, fourteenth to twentieth centuries (see Table 15)

However, the author himself has slightly amended the figures upwards for the first period (1780–90) and Morineau argues convincingly in favour of a further rise in both periods to bring them over 2,000 calories,[9] maintaining that the availability of food in France from the end of Louis XIV's reign to that of Louis Philippe was sufficient, if stationary. If we stretch a little the results shown in Figure 15 and the indications given in source studies – such as those relating to Norfolk day-labourers in the fourteenth and fifteenth centuries, to royal serfs in Sweden in the sixteenth century, or to farmhands in Languedoc in the fifteenth and sixteenth centuries – we can say that food availability in the earlier periods seems to have been abundant and, indeed, to have far exceeded the required levels. The lowest levels, close to the minimum requirement, are to be found at the end of the eighteenth and beginning of the nineteenth centuries in France and England. More convincing than this rather hazardous comparison is the verification, based on a variety of indicators, of a deterioration in both standard of living and food availability in the seventeenth and eighteenth centuries in various parts of Europe, including Sweden and Germany.[10]

Some results relating to Italy in the last four decades of the nineteenth century and to its three main regional subdivisions on the eve of the Second World War, reveal the existence of periods (1880–1900) and areas (Central Italy) with quite low food availability even though food had ceased to be the major problem.

Were we to heed these soundings, European agriculture would be absolved of the accusation of having starved its populations, at least in periods free of catastrophe. But we are dealing only with soundings.

Bread and meat

I have already dwelt in chapter three on the importance of cereals as a source of food among populations during the *ancien régime*. It is worth recalling that the predominance of cereals is easily explained by their durability, their culinary versatility and above all their cheapness. Calorie for calorie, bread is much less expensive than meat or fish, eggs or cheese; in short, than almost all the foods present on the European tables of the past. This is well illustrated by Table 16 which relates, according to the Florentine prices for the period 1610–19, the 'cost' per 1,000 calories of a series of foodstuffs. Setting wheat at 100, only wine (nutritionally valuable only in small quantities), oil (only used as a condiment) and beans (fairly rare at that time) had a cost-

Table 16 *Unit price per 1,000 calories for a number of foodstuffs in Florence, 1600–19*

Foods	Price in gms. of silver	Unit of measure	Price in gms. of silver per edible kg.	Calories per edible kg.	Price in gms. of silver per 1,000 calories Values	Index (Wheat = 100)
Wheat	73.37	hl.	1.012[a]	3,190	0.317	100
Dried beans	79.12	hl.	1.055[b]	3,340	0.316	100
Wine	79.584	hl.	0.796	3,140	0.254	80
Oil	2.754	l.	3.0294[c]	9,000	0.337	106
Veal	3.994	kg.	4.930[d]	920	5.356	1,690
Beef	2.751	kg.	3.439[d]	2,140	1.607	507
Lamb	3.331	kg.	4.164[d]	1,010	4.123	1,301
Mutton	4.147	kg.	5.184[d]	2,260	2.294	724
Local cheese	4.83	kg.	4.830	3,650	1.323	417
Parmesan	8.44	kg.	8.440	3,740	2.257	712
Eggs	3.005	doz.	3.339[e]	1,560	2.14	675
Tench	7.25	kg.	13.182[f]	760	17.345	5,472
Pickled tuna	4.851	kg.	4.851	1,030	4.71	1,485
Sugar	13.795	kg.	13.795	1,920	3.519	1,100
Refined sugar	24.656	kg.	24.656	3,920	6.29	1,984

[a] 72.5000 kg. per hl. (see G. Parenti, *Prime ricerche sulla rivoluzione dei prezzi in Firenze* (Florence, 1939), Appendix 1, p. 78).
[b] 75 kg. per hl.
[c] 1 l. = 1.1 kg.
[d] Edible part put at 80 per cent
[e] One dozen = 0.9 kg.
[f] Edible part put at 55 per cent

calorie equivalence. Cheese costs between four and seven times as much; meats between five and seventeen times, eggs seven times, fresh fish fifty-five times, pickled fish fifteen times, and sugar ten to twenty times as much according to the degree of refinement. These data are, of course, to a large extent indicative, and vary from place to place and from period to period in so far as relative prices changed. Different results are obtained, for example, if the cost per gram of protein, another sensitive indicator, is taken as a basis. However, I shall limit myself to this first comparison as the nutritional problems of the past were doubtless more caloric-quantitative than caloric-qualitative. The undisputable popularity of wheat or other cereals as the primary food and, to a lesser extent, of wine and other alcoholic drinks in the maintenance of a precarious calorie intake is, then, easily explained. Furthermore, cereals were a very important item in the composition of family budgets. To take two examples among many: in prosperous Antwerp at the end of the sixteenth century, about four-fifths of income was spent on food and half on bread.[11] Three centuries later a series of family budget surveys carried out in various provinces in Italy between 1890 and 1906 showed that the proportion of the total food bill spent on bread and cereals varied between a minimum of 52 per cent and a maximum of 95 per cent.[12] In terms of caloric contribution to the energy intake this was never under half and normally lay between two-thirds and three-quarters. Toutain's estimates for France put this figure at over 70 per cent from 1780 to the middle of the nineteenth century, when it declines below this level.[13] In Italy, during the decades that followed Unification, cereals contributed about 60 per cent to the energy intake of the population.[14]

The dietary well-being of the populations of Europe did, then, depend to a large extent on the availability of cereals. Table 17 and Figure 14 show the results of research on the consumption or availability of bread and cereals. One can quote many other literary sources which indicate the abundance of the rations considered normal: a choenix per day (equal to 1,083 litres) was the standard ration in ancient Greece;[15] fifty-one modii per year (equal to 1,219 litres per day) was the ration for an industrious adult slave, according to Cato.[16] These quantities are not very different from the daily kilogram often recorded in later sources.

The data of Table 17, obtained from a variety of sources and by a variety of methods, show that a daily availability of bread or cereals[17] above half a kilo was, by and large, the norm in past centuries. Only the figures for England and Holland fall significantly below this level

Population and nutrition

Table 17 Daily per capita supply of bread and cereals, in grams, in Europe, fourteenth to nineteenth centuries

No.	Place	Period	Categories	Quantity
1	Sweden	1573	Royal serf	900 (Cereals)
2	England (Hunstanton)	1342	Day labourers (harvest)	1,300 (Bread)
3	England (Sedgeford)	1424	Day labourers	700 (Bread)
4	England	1826	Population	260 (Bread)
5	Poland (Nowe Miasto)	1560–70	Royal serfs	620 (Bread)
6	Poland	1500s	Day labourers	1,000 (Bread)
7	Russia	1896–1915	Peasants	699 (Bread)
8	Germany	1500s	Day labourers	1,200 (Bread)
9	Holland	1798	Population	325 (Cereals)
10	France (Languedoc)	1480	Farmworkers	1,150 (Cereals)
11	France (Languedoc)	1580–90	Farmworkers	1,440 (Cereals)
12	France (Gevaudan)	1754–67	Peasants	713–767 (Bread)
13	France (Toulouse)	1700s	Population	689 (Cereals)
14	France (Paris)	1600s–1800s	Population	450–600 (Bread)
15	France	1781–90	Population	552–704 (Bread)
16	France	1803–12	Population	551 (Bread)
17	Italy (Florence)	1338	Population	712 (Cereals)
18	Italy (Genoa)	1382	Population	685 (Bread)
19	Italy (Pavia)	1500s	Population	583–687 (Cereals)
20	Italy (Bologna)	1593	Population	510 (Cereals)
21	Italy (Bologna)	1787–96	Population	545 (Cereals)
22	Italy (Parma)	1500s	Population	600 (Minimum, cereals)
23	Italy (Modena)	1500s	Population	650 (Cereals)
24	Italy (Rome)	Late 1500s	Population	795 (Cereals)
25	Italy (Rome)	1600s	Population	641 (Cereals)
26	Italy (Rome)	1700s	Population	473 (Cereals)
27	Italy (Sicily)	1688–1705	Farmworkers	793 (Cereals)
28	Italy (Sicily)	1681–6	Urban population	682 (Cereals)

29	Italy (near Siena)	1600s	Rural population	700–900 (Bread)
30	Italy (Piedmont)	1700s	Rural population	800 (Cereals)
31	Italy	1861–70	Population	494 (Cereals)
32	Italy	1871–80	Population	543 (Cereals)
33	Italy (North)	1885	Industrial workers	656 (Bread)
34	Italy (Central)	1885	Industrial workers	720 (Bread)
35	Italy (South)	1885	Industrial workers	1,029 (Bread)
36	Greece	Classical	Population	900 (Cereals)

Sources: Sweden: E. Heckscher, *An Economic History of Sweden* (Cambridge, Mass., Harvard University Press, 1954), pp. 69, 116, 149; England (Hunstanton and Sedgeford): C. Dyer, 'Changes in Nutrition and Standard of Living in England 1200–1550', *Ninth Economic History Congress* (Bern, 1986); England: J. C. Drummond and A. Wilbraham, *The Englishman's Food. A History of Five Centuries of English Diet* (London, 1939), p. 46; A. Wyczanski, 'La consommation alimentaire en Pologne', p. 46; Poland (Nowe Miasto): A. Wyczanski, 'La nourriture en Europe Centrale au début de l'Age Moderne', *Ninth Economic History Congress* (Bern, 1986); Russia: B. Kerblay, 'L'évolution de l'alimentation rurale en Russie en 1896–1960', *Pour une histoire de l'alimentation*, J. J. Hémardinquer (ed.), *Cahiers des Annales*, 28 (1970), 46; Germany: A. Wyczanski and M. Dembinska, *La nourriture en Europe Centrale*; Holland: H. Neveux, 'L'alimentation du XIVème au XVIIIème siècle', *Revue d'Histoire Economique et Sociale*, 51 (1973), no. 3, p. 376; France (Languedoc): E. Le Roy Ladurie, *Les Paysans de Languedoc*, p. 267; France (Toulouse): G. Vedel, 'La consommation alimentaire dans le haut Languedoc au XVIIème siècle', *Annales ESC*, 30 (1975), nos. 2–3, p. 489; France (Gevaudan and Paris): H. Neveux, *L'alimentation*, p. 376; France: J.-C. Toutain, 'La consommation alimentaire en France de 1789 à 1964', *Economie et Société*, Cahier de l'ISEA, vol. A, no. 11 (Geneva, 1971); Italy 1977: Italy (Florence and Pavia): D. Zanetti, *Problemi alimentari di una economia pre-industriale* (Turin, 1964), pp. 60–1; Italy (Genoa): J. Day, 'Prix agricoles en Méditerranée à la fin du XIVème siècle', *Annales ESC*, 16 (1965), no. 3, P. 638; Italy (Bologna): A. Guenzi, 'Consumi alimentari e popolazione a Bologna nell'età moderna', *La demografia storica delle città italiane* (Società Italiana di Demografia Storica, Bologna, 1982), pp. 333–4; Italy (Parma): M. A. Romani, *Nella spirale di una crisi* (Milan, 1975), p. 140; Italy (Modena): G. L. Basini, *L'uomo e il pane* (Milan, 1970), p. 50; Italy (Sicily): M. Aymard capital: l'approvisionnement de Rome à l'époque moderne', *Annales ESC*, 30 (1975), nos. 2–3, P. 560; Italy (Rome): J. Revel, 'Les privilèges d'une senese', *Quaderni Storici* (1972), pp. 781–826; Italy (Piedmont): G. Prato, *La vita economica in Piemonte a mezzo il secolo XVIII* and J. Bresc, *Nourritures et consommation*; Italy (near Siena): O. Di Simplicio, 'Due secoli di produzione agraria in una fattoria (Turin, 1908), p. 438; Italy (1861–80): ISTAT, *Statistiche storiche dell'Italia 1861–1975* (Rome, 1976), p. 159; Italy (1885): S. Somogyi, 'L'alimentazione nell'Italia unita', *Storia d'Italia*, vol. V (Turin, 1973). p. 849; Greece: L. Gallo, *Alimentazione e demografia della Grecia antica* (Salerno, 1984), p. 31. A normal ration was held to be a choenix, equivalent to 1,083 litres.

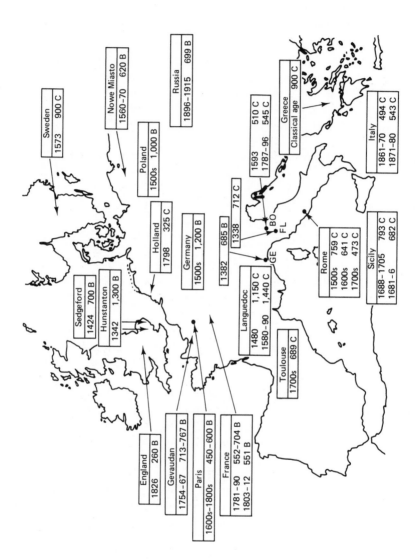

Figure 14 Daily per capita consumption of bread and cereals in certain
European zones, fourteenth to twentieth centuries (see Table 17)

at the beginning of the nineteenth century. In these cases, however, we are dealing with populations which were reasonably well fed and among which the potato had largely taken the place of bread, particularly in Holland. Rations of a kilogram or more were fairly frequent, particularly in earlier periods. In Italian cities between the fourteenth and the eighteenth centuries, or in non-urban areas around Siena and in Sicily in the seventeenth century, or in eighteenth-century Piedmont, availability of bread ranged usually between 500 and 800 grams per day. If we take the lower value – 500 grams of bread per day – the caloric input is roughly 1,250 calories, while 500 grams of wheat equal 1,600 calories. These are respectively two-thirds or over three-quarters of the hypothetical daily requirement of 2,000 calories. So, for example, a half-kilo loaf of bread (1,250 calories), complemented by 100 grams of black olives (250 calories), 100 grams of cheese (400 calories), half an onion and the odd fruit or vegetable in season would have satisfied the 'average' requirement, and has constituted the most normal diet of Mediterranean countries from the time of Homer until virtually the present day.

It would be unwise to press our inductions further as this might lead us into a kind of *false precision*,[18] always to be avoided in a case like this where the phenomena are so variable and described so imprecisely.

If the estimates on bread availability for the communities and periods for which such estimates exist would seem to indicate a sufficient, if rather monotonous, diet, we must remember that they related only to normal years, free of famine. According to Galiani,[19] the availability of cereals in the Kingdom of Naples never fell below the average by more than 25 per cent in the worst years. It is obvious, however, that food shortages resulting from poor harvests combined with price increases and the consequent social disruption, had multiplicative effects on the less well-off.

Thus, judging by the consumption of cereals and bread, a sufficient caloric intake seems to have been easily fulfilled in normal times by anyone living in non-marginal circumstances. But what can be said about the quality of the diet? Strictly speaking, this could only be assessed through a detailed examination of the nutritional components normally present in everyday food, an operation doomed to failure for the earlier periods. The use of synthetic indicators, however, can put us on the right path. It would be interesting, for instance, to know what proportion of the total calories available or ingested were of animal origin, or something about consumption of proteins, particularly those from animal sources. But these simple indications can only be found for recent periods, and even so they are only approximate.

We can assume that the consumption of meat was correlated with the indicators discussed above, and some rough estimates do exist. There is an authoritative and 'strong' hypothesis which holds that meat consumption was relatively high during the last two centuries of the Middle Ages and until the latter part of the sixteenth century, that it declined gradually to a minimum somewhere around the beginning of the nineteenth century, and that it began to rise again during the course of that century – and in some areas only in the twentieth century – though at a different pace in different countries. The chief exponent of this theory is Abel,[20] partly in the wake of Schmoller's studies in the last century. The *Wustungen* process (abandonment of land) reinforced by the plague cycle of the Middle Ages underlay the conversion to grazing of wide tracts of land previously given over to crops, and so to the increasing practice of stock-breeding and meat-eating. In late medieval Germany, according to Abel, the normal consumption per head exceeded 100 kg., but the crises of later centuries depressed this figure to a low of 14 kg. at the beginning of the nineteenth century. In Abel's own words,

the demand for cereals is relatively inelastic. It varies with variations in the population, and since in the late Middle Ages . . . this dwindled, so did the demand for cereals. The demand for meat is, on the other hand, elastic. It varies with variations in income, so that the increased purchasing power of a wide spectrum of consumers between the end of the fourteenth and the beginning of the fifteenth century was to reabsorb, to no negligible extent, a reduced demand due to the contraction in the number of consumers, and to push it in the direction of meat products.[21]

The high level of meat consumption in medieval Germany, and its later downward trend, seem to be substantiated by information on England and Holland. Sir John Fortescue in the fifteenth century commented about the English: 'They eat plentifully of all kinds of flesh and fish.'[22] The abundance of meat at their table, as well as its gradual decline in later centuries, seems beyond doubt. Meat consumption in fourteenth- and fifteenth-century Italy was also rather high, at least in Piedmont[23] and Sicily.[24] 'Herds and flocks were a common sight in medieval Italy, encouraged by the existence of large free tracts of land at a time of declining population and therefore low cultivation.'[25] The decline in meat consumption in later periods, with the exception of richer urban areas, is testified to by the low levels of consumption which prevailed well into the twentieth century. In the rest of Europe as well, consumption seems to have declined from the sixteenth century, though from initially lower levels. In certain areas, however, meat consumption remained relatively high, for example in England and Flanders and perhaps in parts of eastern Europe.[26] We can also guess that traditionally stock-raising areas with a regular export trade, like the Tyrol, Switzerland, Denmark, southern Sweden and, further east, Hungary, Podolia, Moldavia and Walachia,[27] had higher than average consumption. Moreover, the increase in livestock export from East to West after the fifteenth century is due in part to the abandonment of stock-raising in the West, as a response to the pressure of demographic growth, so that not even the modest and declining demand for meat could be met with local products.[28] At the end of the seventeenth century, Gregory King estimated that in England, out of a population of five and a half million, 1.6 million ate meat every day, 0.7 million ate it five times a week, 3.0 million once a week and 0.2 million never.[29] It is thought that the average annual consumption at that time in England was around 33 kg. per head,[30] considerably lower than the German 100 kg. two to three centuries earlier, but double that estimated for the beginning of the nineteenth century. The long-term trend for the consumption of other animal-derived products such as butter, eggs, cheese and lard was similar, as it was, too, for game.[31]

That meat consumption was very low over large areas of Europe in the last century is a well-documented fact. According to Toutain's estimates, it did not exceed 20 kg. a year in France between 1780 and 1834, and only after this latter date did it again begin to increase.[32] The estimates for post-Unification Italy are even lower: 13 kg. between 1861–70, and barely 2 kg. more in 1901–10, reaching 30 kg. a year only in the 1930s.[33] In spring 1787, while travelling in Sicily, Goethe and his companions were able to stock up liberally on artichokes and the like along the way, but on reaching Caltanissetta were puzzled as to where to cook a hen purchased *en route* – an anecdotal indication of the Sicilians' unfamiliarity with meat at the time.[34] For rural populations in Italy, as for much of the Mediterranean, meat was a rare luxury, often reserved for feast-days until well into the twentieth century. Reduced mortality occurred independently of the increased consumption of meat.

Table 18 gives estimates of annual meat consumption per head in kilograms for a number of non-selected European communities between the fourteenth and nineteenth centuries. Abel's assumption is not disproven, and the lower levels of consumption in the Mediterranean basin are quite apparent. We are no doubt justified in asking how a satisfactory measure of the contributions made by domestic

Population and nutrition

Table 18 *Meat consumption (Yearly kg. per head) in Europe, fourteenth to nineteenth centuries*

No.	Place	Period	Population studied	kg.
1	Sweden	1573	Royal serfs	100
2	England (Hunstanton)	1342	Rural	73
3	England (Sedgeford)	1424	Rural	219
4	England	1400s	Peasants	72
5	England	1600s	Population	33
6	England (London)	1700s	Population	83
7	Poland	1500s	Rural population	16
8	Germany	1400s	Population	100
9	Germany (Saxony)	1500s	Rural population	12
10	Germany	1700s	Population	14
11	Holland (towns)	1801–4	Population	24
12	Holland (rural)	1801–4	Population	31
13	France (Carpentras)	1400s	Population	26
14	France (Languedoc)	1480	Farmworkers	40
15	France (Tours)	1476–82	Population	43
16	France (Gevaudan)	1700s	Rural population	2–10
17	France (Toulouse)	1700s	Population	16
18	France (Verfeil)	1700s	Population	16
19	France	1781–90	Population	19
20	France	1803–12	Population	20
21	France	1855–64	Population	30
22	Switzerland (Geneva)	1700s	Population	80
23	Italy (Palermo)	1452–3	Population	16–26
24	Italy (Castrogiovanni)	1449–50	Population	20–6
25	Italy (Sicily)	1500s	Village population	2–10
26	Italy (Bologna)	1593	Population	46
27	Italy (Bologna)	1787–96	Population	35
28	Italy (Rome)	1600s	Population	31–8
29	Italy (Palermo)	1648–60	Population	14
30	Italy (Sicily)	1720	Village population	2–10
31	Italy (Rome)	1770–90	Population	21–9
32	Italy	1861–70	Population	13
33	Spain (Valladolid)	1500s	Population	34–7
34	Spain (Oviedo)	1500s	Population	27
35	Spain (Castille)	1500s	Village population	2–10

Sources: Sweden: E. Heckscher, *An Economic History of Sweden* (Cambridge, Mass., Harvard University Press, 1954), p. 1; England (Hunstanton and Sedgeford): C. Dyer, 'Changes in Nutrition and Standard of Living in England, 1200–1550', *Ninth Economic History Congress* (Bern, 1986); England (1400s): J. C. Drummond and E. A. Wilbraham, *The Englishman's Food. A History of Five Centuries of English Diet* (London, 1939), p. 465; England (1600s): Gregory King's estimates in H. Neveux, 'L'alimentation du XIVème au XVIIIème siècle', *Revue d'Histoire Economique et Sociale*, 51 (1973), no. 3, p. 360;

livestock holdings, game reserves and fishing would alter this picture: for one thing, fishing must have significantly enriched the diets of coastal populations and those living near rivers or lakes.

New crops. Did diet improve in the eighteenth century?

The influence of new cereal crops like buckwheat and more especially maize, of tubers like the potato, of pulses like peas and beans, all of which spread quite rapidly throughout Europe from the seventeenth century onwards, made an impact on the eating habits of European populations.[35] The role played by these new crops, particularly by the potato in central and northern Europe, and by maize in southern Europe, was twofold. On the one hand, they increased the yield per unit of land, a fact of considerable importance given Europe's expanded population; and on the other, they diversified harvests, making these as a whole less vulnerable to climatic fluctuations.[36] An area of land planted with potatoes could feed twice or three times as many people as if it had been planted with cereal,[37] if not four times the number according to Arthur Young's observations in Ireland.[38] Similarly, maize yields per unit of land were much higher than wheat yields.[39] The more versatile buckwheat could be sown late in the season should winter wheat have failed.[40] By the latter part of the eighteenth century the potato had conquered Europe. The serious famine which descended on central-northern Europe between 1770–2 gave momentum to its diffusion[41] and encouraged the reluctant to overcome their suspicion or dislike of it.

Maize spread through Spain during the seventeenth century, passing then to south-west France and northern Italy, particularly Lombardy, the Veneto and Emilia, progressing thence to the Balkans.[42] As with the potato after the 1770–2 famine, the 1816–17 subsistence crisis stimulated farmers to put more land under maize cultivation.[43]

The adoption of these new crops did not necessarily entail an

Poland: A. Wyczanski and M. Dembinska, 'La nourriture en Europe Centrale au début de l'Age Moderne', *Ninth Economic History Congress* (Bern, 1986); Holland: Neveux, 'L'alimentation', p. 360; France (1700s and 1800s): J.-C. Toutain, 'La consommation alimentaire en France de 1789 à 1964', *Economie et Société*, Cahier de l'ISEA, vol. A, no. 11 (Geneva, 1971), p. 194; Italy (Bologna): A. Guenzi, 'Consumi alimentari e popolazione a Bologna nell'età moderna', p. 36; Italy (1800s): ISTAT, *Statistiche Storiche dell'Italia 1861–1975* (Rome, 1976), 'Sommario', p. 159; Other areas: B. Benassar and J. Goy, 'Contribution à l'histoire de la consommation alimentaire', pp. 421–3.

increase in availability per head. Many authors emphasise that the demographic expansion of the eighteenth century became a running battle between population and resources, in Ireland as in France, in Germany as in England.[44] In Ireland Connell states, 'as potatoes were substituted for the traditional foodstuffs, a family's subsistence could be found from a diminished section of its holding'.[45] Relinquishing the cultivation of cereals did not impair the quality of nutrition, but probably it did not improve it either, though Cobbett's invective against the potato as a result of his travels in Ireland is perhaps exaggerated:

I will never give constant employment to any man in whose garden I shall see potatoes planted . . . it is both my pleasure and my duty to discourage in any way I can the cultivation of this damned root, being convinced that it has done more harm to mankind than the sword and the pestilence united.[46]

It has been estimated that in Great Britain and Ireland, wheat consumption per head dropped from 680 grams a day around 1765 to 408 grams in 1835. At the same time, potato consumption in England and Wales doubled.[47] In Flanders, as the potato rose in popularity the consumption of cereals was almost halved within a century, from 893 grams per head per day in 1693 to 475 grams in 1791.[48] This pattern repeated itself in Lombardy, the Veneto and Emilia, with maize taking the place of the higher quality cereals during the last century,[49] as it had in south-west France between the mid-eighteenth and mid-nineteenth centuries.[50]

The role of the new crops in the composition of diets and their demographic effects are, then, clear. On the one hand, they led to higher productivity and more stable production and thus reduced the impact of crises – although the experience of Ireland tells us that the crisis was actually magnified by dependence on the potato; on the other hand, demographic expansion largely undermined the positive effects of greater availability. In more than one case the substitution of a diet with a lower caloric content per unit of weight led to a deterioration in the overall nutritional level. Although currently out of fashion, R. N. Salaman's classical opinion is that

in its early days the potato saved the Irish people in their time of greatest danger; later, by stabilising the life of the masses at the lowest standard consistent with their continued physical existence, it gradually rendered them more or less indifferent to 'the slings and arrows of outrageous fortune'.[51]

Indeed, if we take a good look at this, it seems but a restatement of the vicious circle of interdependence between resources and population. The putting of new land under cultivation, which gained momentum everywhere in the eighteenth century, came partly as a result of the demographic boom and the ensuing rise in cereal prices. Increased demand is met by the increased amount of land put under the plough and the introduction of new and better-yield crops which take the place of more expensive and better quality products.

Drawing together the disparate threads of our discussion, are we able to gain an overall view of the levels and trends of nutrition among European populations? Taking into account the existence of dietary models and levels from a wide variety of geographical regions, I shall hazard a hypothesis – which seems to be supported by scholarly opinion – along the following lines: there were generous diets with high meat content in the last two centuries of the Middle Ages until well into the sixteenth century; a marked decline in meat consumption until the nineteenth century, although the basic caloric requirement was met in years of normality; malnutrition in recurrent years of famine, especially until the eighteenth century; lesser hardship in times of want from the second half of the eighteenth century, due in part to the development of trade and new crops, but with 'normal' levels of consumption generally stationary; widespread progress during the nineteenth century which, however, does not reach fringe areas such as the Balkans or the Mediterranean, until well into the twentieth century. These trends make themselves felt at different times and in varying degrees; for instance, almost all the literature points to England's greater prosperity even in times of lesser plenty.

This rapid summary needs to be extended. The theory, held by many and pushed to its limits by McKeown,[52] that the demographic growth and decline in mortality that took place in the eighteenth century was a result of dietary improvements, probably has a grain of truth in it but needs further proof. After all, is it true that dietary conditions improved so much in the second half of the eighteenth and the beginning of the nineteenth centuries so as to lead to a reduction in the mortality rate in a number of populations? We have already seen that as far as meat consumption went, there was no improvement. And there are other voices of dissent. According to Morineau, from the end of Louis XIV's reign to that of Louis Philippe the French enjoyed an adequate if monotonous diet, except during famines. Between 1750 and 1840, cereal yields remained constant on the whole, and the increment in land put under cultivation for food production went in step with the growth in population without increasing availability per head. The success of the potato in eastern

France and of maize in the south-west served, if anything, to compensate for the decline in the relative availability of cereals.[53] It is a point of view that basically fits in with the Malthusian model: the availability of new land through drainage, the turning over of pastures to crop-growing, and deforestation combined with greater yield per unit of land – as had occurred in Ireland and other areas with the adoption of the potato – to stimulate the formation of new households and encourage demographic growth, rather than improve the quantity or quality of food.[54] In this formulation, however, the demographic cycle operates through stimuli and checks on marriage rather than on mortality.

Similar conclusions can be drawn for England and Wales between the mid-eighteenth century and the end of the Napoleonic Wars. The price paid during a century of industrialisation in terms of deteriorating standards of living both for farming and for factory or city populations was a hard one.[55] The population grew a good deal faster than agricultural production and England, from being a net exporter, became a net importer of foodstuffs between the first and second half of the eighteenth century.[56] Total consumption, including food, which certainly improved during the first half of the eighteenth century, stagnated if not regressed in the second half of the century to the end of the Napoleonic wars.[57] It is commonly held that this marked improvement in food consumption compared with the seventeenth century gave way to a deterioration in the second part of the eighteenth century.[58] Tension did not diminish even with the onset of the nineteenth century, at least for the population in the south, traditionally dependent on grain consumption. 'The southern labourers endured the full force of overpopulation, the enclosures and the corn laws';[59] so much so that for wheat-eaters, whose number increased both absolutely and proportionally, wheat consumption per head actually dropped between 1801 and 1850.[60]

In Sweden, improvements in the level of nutrition became apparent only from the mid-nineteenth century onwards, that is to say three-quarters of a century after the decline in mortality had begun. As we shall see, real wages stagnated and the practice of extending the areas under cultivation seems to have brought about a change in the flow of foodstuffs, rather than an increase in consumption per head. Thus, between the early 1800s and 1860, Sweden, from being an importer, became an exporter of cereals.[61] There are also signs of worsening mortality rates due to tuberculosis, a phenomenon which does not agree with the hypothesis of improved standards of nutrition.[62]

In Piedmont, the level of consumption was fair in the mid-eighteenth century but does not appear to have risen much until the beginning of the twentieth century. The consumption of some foods, such as cereals, increased but that of others, such as wine, decreased.[63] In some areas, as for instance around Vercelli, worsening standards of living are actually recorded during the second half of the eighteenth and the first decades of the nineteenth centuries.[64] In Spain 'the increase in farming production during the eighteenth century could not keep pace with the growth in population, and the relationship between subsistence and population undoubtedly grew worse during the course of that century'. Things began to improve only in the middle of the following one.[65]

In other words, more than one reasonable doubt exists as to the extent, or even existence, of dietary improvement before the nineteenth century. Also, even if some improvement did occur it was not sizeable enough to return nutritional levels to those of 1350–1550, defined by Braudel as the 'happy period'. To this he adds that

the deterioration was intensified as the 'medieval autumn' set in, and was to last till the middle of the nineteenth century, whereas in eastern Europe the decline continued, especially in the Balkans, right into the twentieth century.[66]

The standard of living and real wages

Our knowledge of the nutritional habits of the Europeans provides a hazy picture in which qualitative appraisals of levels or trends predominate over quantitative ones. Several threads useful to the argument we are laboriously weaving are provided by the long historical series of prices and wages which exist for many European countries. The prices that concern us most are those of cereals, particularly of wheat with which the prices of other cereals are closely correlated. We have already seen that about two-thirds of the energy requirement of preindustrial populations was provided by cereals. Nutritional well-being can, therefore, be expressed in terms of the availability or consumption of cereals. Wages are usually those earned by farm hands or craftsmen in the building or manufacturing trades. Real wages series, obtained by dividing the index for money wages by the price index for cereals (or other more complex indices like that of Phelps Brown and Hopkins in England), are certainly a possible indicator of variations in the standard of living of populations, or of their purchasing power for cereals, but they have serious limitations which it is well to consider.

In the first place, prices reflect the money value of marketed foods which represented only a part, and not the main part, of consumption. Barter, and above all self-consumption by the producer, was the rule in most rural populations.[67] In the second place, wages usually reflected the earnings of only a section of the working population, namely hired workmen in towns and farm labourers who did not own land. Yet even for these categories real wages did not necessarily represent the real income trend and therefore the purchasing power of these families. We know little or nothing about the amount and variation of payments in kind, which were frequent;[68] nor about the additions to the money or food budget made by other members of the family or by other supplementary activities; nor about the trends in employment, unemployment or length of employment; nor, finally, about the contributions to nutritional balance made by vegetable plots, common land, woods, game and fishing.

'At Heilbron', Goethe records, 'the roads and alleys along the walls and away from the main road, were used by every small householder as a depository for manure'[69] which they evidently used to cultivate their allotments on neighbouring land. The French consumption survey of 1967 showed that about one-half of households resorted to produce of one kind or another from their allotments, kitchen gardens or small fields – and this in a highly urbanised and industrialised society.[70] Even today the outskirts of Italian cities are scattered with small kitchen gardens where every free shred of ground which has escaped the process of urbanisation is cultivated with fruit and vegetables. One can imagine that in a society which was almost exclusively rural and much less densely populated than nowadays, this phenomenon must have been more widespread. This was certainly the case in the High Middle Ages when 'the kitchen garden . . . constituted an important economic reality, and spread everywhere as though by capillary action'.[71]

With these reservations, the course of real wages earned by hired workmen may be taken as a reasonable indicator of their standard of living; but to take them as indicators of the standard of living for farmers, whether land-owning, sharecropping or tenant, among whom self-consumption was the rule is more hazardous still. We may take another example from our own century: before the October revolution, about four-fifths of the food consumed by Russian peasants was self-produced and only one-fifth was bought on the market.[72] From the point of view of the producers, the Physiocrats' dictum would fit the bill: 'Abondance et non valeur n'est pas richesse. Disette et cherté est misère. Abondance et cherté est opulence'

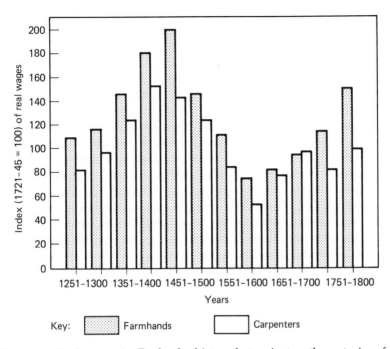

Figure 15 Real wages in England, thirteenth to nineteenth centuries, for farmhands and carpenters
Source: B. J. Slicher Van Bath, *Storia agraria dell'Europa Occidentale (1500–1850)* (Turin, 1972), p. 247.

['Plenty and cheapness is not wealth. Dearth and high prices is poverty. Plenty and high prices is opulence']. In any case it is not clear what a decline in real wages might actually mean to producers.

Keeping these points in mind – which I have made not to forestall criticism but to help in the interpretation of the indicators – let us now look at Figure 15 which shows the course of real wages (expressed in wheat) in England for farm labourers and carpenters from the thirteenth to nineteenth centuries, as calculated by Abel. Over this long period the index is very high in the two centuries following the Black Death, it falls sharply in the second half of the sixteenth century, recovers in the second half of the seventeenth and first half of the eighteenth, plummeting again in the second half of the eighteenth before starting its long ascent at the beginning of the nineteenth century. Records of prices and real wages relating to other European countries are very numerous and confirm along broad lines the findings in Figure 15: increase in real wages during the century after the first outbreak of the plague; decrease during the sixteenth century, recovery in the seventeenth, and another slump in the second part of the eighteenth century. Although this was the basic pattern, there were of course regional differences in timing and in the severity or mildness of local conditions, proving yet again that one must beware of generalisations. The periods of declining populations caused by the plague, as in the fourteenth and fifteenth centuries, accompanied sometimes by other catastrophes as in the seventeenth century, are periods of low demand for food, falling prices and a shrinking labour-force, with a consequent rise in wages. In Germany, according to Franz, the Thirty Years War reduced rural populations by 40 per cent and urban ones by a third.[73] In 1653, a local farmer complained: 'only the servants are still contented and well-tempered, we almost have to surrender our purses to them and serve them hand and foot, while we starve'.[74] Even after these surprising effects disappeared, wages remained high.

Figure 16, taken from Abel, confirms the trends outlined for a number of European countries in the sixteenth and eighteenth centuries – two centuries in which wages rose much less than did the prices for food and other commodities, whether in Germany, France, England or Poland.

The purpose of this brief look at price and wage movements is to find out whether it can help us to answer our central question, namely whether mortality trends (from what can be gleaned) followed the real wage trends, rising when the standard of living declined and declining when it rose. Unfortunately, the data needed to test this are scanty, but what we can put together gives a surprising picture. In Figure 17, which relates to England, a more elaborate index of real wages (in fact the Phelps Brown and Hopkins index, which incidentally also confirms the trends in Figure 16) is shown together with the life expectancy trend worked out by Wrigley and Schofield for the period 1541–1849, using broad twenty-five-year averages. The surprise is that the two phenomena are connected by a clearcut *inverse* relationship: life expectancy rises in the sixteenth century until the first quarter of the seventeenth, while wages go down; the subsequent decline of life expectancy, reaching troughs in the last quarter of the seventeenth and the second quarter of the eighteenth century, coincides with steadily increasing wages, while the decline of the latter between the middle of the eighteenth and the first quarter of the nineteenth centuries coincides with a significant increase in levels of survival.[75] If, then, real wage trends are tied to trends in nutritional level, and this is certainly true for the wage-earning

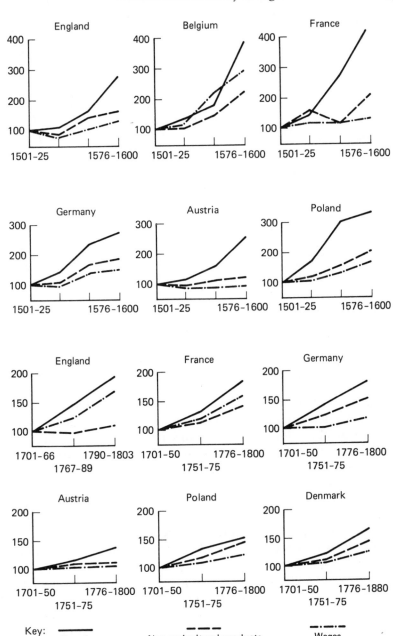

Figure 16 Prices and wages in some European countries in the sixteenth and
eighteenth centuries
Source: Abel, *Congiuntura agraria e crisi agraria* (Turin, 1976), pp. 176 and 297.

Figure 17 Real wages and life expectancy in England, 1541–1850
Source: E. A. Wrigley and R. S. Schofield, *The Population History of England, 1541–1871* (London, 1981), pp. 528 and 642.

population, there appears to be no perceptible direct link, at least in the aggregate, with mortality. If anything, the exact opposite is true.

Unfortunately, long-term estimates for mortality like those that exist for England do not exist for other countries, and we have therefore to content ourselves with a number of indirect indices. For example, the observation that periods of demographic sluggishness – like those of the century after the Black Death of 1348, or the seventeenth century – may be periods of high mortality but are also periods of high purchasing power for wage earners and therefore presumably of greater food availability per head. This situation seems to apply to most of Europe.[76]

This confirms our argument that great epidemic cycles are largely independent of the state of nutrition of populations. This is further substantiated in Figure 18, which shows the value of real wages, taken over fifty-year periods and expressed as bushels of grain purchasable by a builder in Florence with one day's pay, and the frequency of severe mortality crises in some areas of Tuscany, taken over one hundred-year spans for each area observed, between the

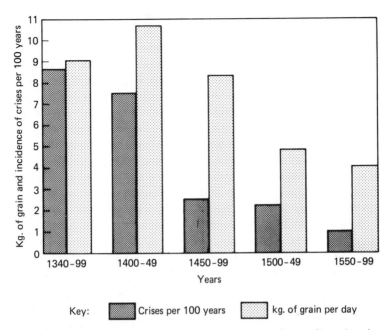

Figure 18 Real wages in Florence and frequency of mortality crises in
Tuscany, fourteenth to sixteenth centuries
Sources: L. Del Panta, *Le epidemie nella storia demografica italiana (secoli XIV—
XIX)* (Turin, 1980), p. 1£32. For 1550–99 our estimates are based on data
drawn from L. Del Panta, 'Cronologia e diffusione', *Ricerche Storiche*, 7
(1977), no. 2. For the real wages series, see R. A. Goldthwaite, *The Building
of Renaissance Florence* (Baltimore, 1980), pp. 439–9.

fourteenth and the sixteenth centuries.[77] Before 1348, a day's wage
enabled the worker to purchase 0.2 or 0.3 bushels of grain. Average
values rise to 0.6 bushels during the first half of the fifteenth century
(with frequent years when the purchasing power reached 1 bushel),
only to fall to 0.2 bushels during the second half of the sixteenth
century. The frequency of the great mortality crises reaches a peak in
the middle of the fifteenth century, when real wages were at their
highest, and then falls away rapidly, reaching a minimum during the
second half of the sixteenth century, when real wages were also at a
minimum.

Yet the plague was devastating and there was little that individual
or social defences – among them the quantity and quality of food –
could do in the face of it. But during the second part of the seventeenth and in the eighteenth century the plague vanished from Italy.

Great mortality crises were often linked with years of bad harvest, of which we have seen many examples. Figure 19 shows real wages for building workers in Milan, expressed in kilograms of bread purchasable with the daily wage, and the relative frequency of mortality crises in north-central Italy, though there is no discernible uniformity of trend. Indeed, the period when wages were at their lowest, 1740–1800, coincides with the period of lowest frequency of mortality crises. Moreover, real wages declined everywhere in the second half of the eighteenth century just when life expectancy began its ascent.

It is true that besides these trends, whether upward or downward, what matters is the level of real wages and their ability to guarantee sufficient purchasing power and an adequate level of nutrition. According to Braudel, until the middle of the sixteenth century, the price of one quintal of grain remained below the wage equivalent of 100 hours of work, and then rose to stay above this level until the second half of the nineteenth century. 'A workman has at his disposal about 3,000 hours of work per year; his family (four people) consumes about twelve quintals of wheat a year. Overstepping 100 hours per quintal is serious, overstepping 200 is alarming, overstepping 300 means famine.'[78] The 200 hour mark was often reached and exceeded in France in the eighteenth century and up to the second decade of the nineteenth by which time mortality declined markedly.[79] In early fourteenth-century Florence a quintal of corn cost a builder's hand between 200 and 300 hours of work, a figure which after the plague fell to 100 hours and often to as little as 50 or 60.[80] In the decade after Italy's unification (1862–9), according to calculations made by the Direzione Generale di Statistica, a factory hand needed to work about 300 hours to purchase a hectolitre of wheat and one of maize (50 per cent cheaper than wheat), therefore overstepping the alarm threshold as defined by Braudel.[81]

It has been observed that my interpretation of the relationship between mortality and real wages, contrary to expectations, is to some degree incorrect.[82] In fact, the trend of real wages depends, essentially, on the trend of prices. These prices increase in periods of demographic growth and decrease in periods of decline, a growth and decline which is often linked to decline or growth in mortality. As a consequence, real wages are dependent on the population trend, and the relationship between these corresponds perfectly with expectations. The logic of this argument, however, is only apparent. If, indeed, wages are also an index of the standard of living, how can mortality decline over long periods in spite of a parallel decline of wages (and vice versa)? This can come about only if the deterioration

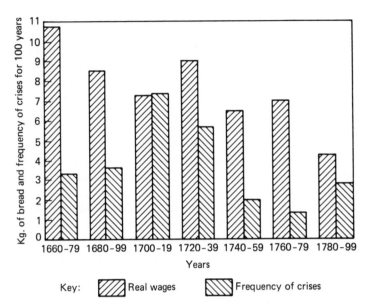

Figure 19 Real wages in Milan and frequency of mortality crises in north-central Italy, seventeenth to eighteenth centuries
Sources: For real wages: G. Vigo, 'Real Wages of the Working Class in Italy: Building Workers' Wages (Fourteenth to Eighteenth Centuries)' in *Journal of European Economic History*, 3 (1974), no. 2, p. 396. For the crises: L. Del Panta, *Le epidemie nella storia demografica italiana (secoli XIV–XIX)* (Turin, 1980), p. 197.

of purchasing power does not imply a deterioration of nutritional levels sufficient to be reflected in mortality, an observation which suggests the relative independence of mortality and indices of material wellbeing. This is just the point which I have been seeking to establish.

A more detailed analysis of the connection, or rather lack of connection, between real wages and mortality would not strengthen my argument. The advocates of a primarily nutritional explanation of the demographic trends of the past encounters, however, one more obstacle to overcome.

Stature, living conditions and food

In the previous sections, I have tried to summarise and organise, for the benefit of demographers, what little is known about trends and levels of nutrition in Europe. From these findings there seems to be little evidence of an improvement in the nutritional situation in the second half of the eighteenth century, and this casts doubt on the belief that the coincident fall in mortality might be attributed to improved diet. Meat consumption reached its lowest point at the beginning of the nineteenth century. Real wages together with the standard of living of large sections of the population deteriorated during the second half of the eighteenth century and remained at a low level during the first years of the nineteenth century. The introduction of new crops, undoubtedly a positive phenomenon, allowed larger populations to be fed but, in many well-documented cases, this did not mean an improvement in the quality of the diet of the masses.

There is still more evidence that can be cited. Recent research has extended our knowledge of certain relevant anthropometric characteristics back into the eighteenth century.[83] If a high proportion of the family budget went on food during the preindustrial age, and if food is an important determining factor in stature, then trends in stature are a good guide to the living conditions of a population. This chain of reasoning is not without its weak links. I shall not, however, enter into a debate which bristles with technical difficulties concerning the validity of sources (usually of military provenance), the comparability of the measurements and the distortion of the samples measured, to name but a few, all of which are dealt with in specialised publications.[84] I shall only comment that height is certainly correlated with nutritional level and reflects its 'net' effect; 'net', that is, of the negative effects that the severity and frequency of infectious disease, the type of physical activity pursued, and other environmental factors can have on the role played by nutrition in body growth.[85] Given equal nutritional levels, for instance, we may expect that a population suffering a higher incidence of childhood diseases – which might be due to poor hygiene or frequency of epidemic attacks – will reach a lower stature than one which observes good rules of hygiene and is not exposed to contagion. Thus, variations in height reflect not only variations in nutrition but also differences in the frequency of contagious diseases, independently of prevailing nutritional habits.[86] The state of the art does not yet enable us to unravel the causal tangle of food–hygiene–infection–height, even in current studies.

With these reservations, the evolution of stature represents an important index of the well-being of a population, particularly if seen in conjunction with other evidence. Some recently discovered data for the eighteenth century hold several surprises. Under the Hapsburg monarchy, the average height of army recruits, aged at least twenty-three years and subdivided by region of birth, seems to decline noticeably between the generations born around the middle of the century or before and those born around its end.[87] Thus, for those born in Hungary, heights went from over 170.1 cm. for the generation of 1740 to 162.1 cm. for that of 1790 and 163.7 cm. for that of 1820; in the case of Lower Austria the following heights are recorded: 164.6 cm. (born 1750), 161.6 cm. (1780) and 163.2 cm. (1790); in the case of Galicia the heights were: 168.6 cm. (1750), 158.8 cm. (1820) and 160.1 cm. (1830); and for Bosnia: 165.3 cm. (1740), 160.8 cm. (1790). These data are shown in Table 19.

In America, by the time of the Revolution, recruits had already reached an average height of 171.6 cm., clearly taller than their European counterparts in the nineteenth century. More surprisingly, this figure remained virtually the same for conscripts during the Civil War (171.9 cm.) and also the Second World War (again 171.9 cm.).[88] Thus, by the middle of the eighteenth century, nutrition in America had evidently reached a satisfactory level – the improvement having taken place, it would seem, earlier in the century.[89] I have already discussed the fact that the high-grade diet of the Americans during the nineteenth century contrasts with a mortality not unlike that of the Europeans.

Returning to Europe, we find trends similar to that of the Hapsburg Empire (about the mortality of which we know little) in Sweden where the height of recruits decreased towards the end of the nineteenth century.[90] The trend in the height of London adolescents of the poorer classes provides evidence of worsening conditions in urban areas: it was stationary between 1770 and 1795 and thereafter declined perceptibly until around 1810, as did urban real wages, before starting on a thirty-year recovery.[91] Similar tendencies are to be found among children and adolescents of various classes in the Austro-Hungarian Empire, where a marked decline in height started around 1760 and lasted until the end of the Napoleonic wars when it began to increase again.[92]

Other authors connect low stature among Germans at the beginning of the nineteenth century, which was lower than the average height in medieval times, with the well-known variations in meat eating, which at that time had reached an all-time low.[93]

Although the inferences to be drawn from these data are not entirely unambiguous, they are nonetheless consistent with what has emerged so far about the stagnation, if not the actual deterioration, of levels of nutrition in the second half of the eighteenth century, and also perhaps in the early part of the nineteenth century. Speaking of

Population and nutrition

Table 19. *Height in cm. of soldiers under the Hapsburg Monarchy by region of birth and in Sweden, generations 1740-1830*

Year of birth	Austro-Hungarian Empire[a]					Kingdom of Sweden[b]
	Hungary	Lower Austria	Galicia	Bohemia	Moravia	
1740	170.1	—	—	165.3	166.3	169.7
1750	168.6	164.6	168.9	164.4	165.8	170.7
1760	167	—	167.2	163.4	—	170.9
1770	162.5	163.1	163.7	161.5	—	170.9
1780	163.3	161.6	164.2	163.8	—	170.8
1790	162.1	163.2	—	160.8	—	170.7
1800	163	—	—	—	—	171.1
1810	165	—	—	—	—	171.7
1820	163.7	—	158.8	—	—	172.7
1830	—	—	160.1	—	—	173.5

[a]Minimum age of conscripts: 23 years
[b]Conscripts 25–29 years of age. Values derived from a graph estimating the underlying trend. The empiric series is stationary in the eighteenth century, with dips in the eighties and nineties.
Sources: For the Hapsburg Monarchy: J. Komlos, 'Stature and Nutrition in the Habsburg Monarchy: the Standard of Living and Economic Development in the Eighteenth Century', *The American Historical Review*, 90 (1985), no. 5, p. 1155; For Sweden: L. G. Sandberg and R. H. Steckel, 'Soldier, Soldier, What Made You Grow so Tall?', *Economy and History*, 23 (1980), no. 2, p. 98.

Europe, however, it is necessary to emphasise once again the great geographic variations in levels and trends and the imprecision which attends all generalisations. It is worth noting, with Tanner, that another biological phenomenon associated with levels of nutrition, namely age at puberty, seems to remain constant during the greater part of the nineteenth century both in Germany and in England, yet another indication of the less than overwhelming evolution of diets.[94]

6

Antagonism and adaptation

Constraints and biological adaptation

The vicissitudes of Europe's populations – as, indeed, those of all populations in all periods – have been dominated by continuous friction between the forces of constraint and the capacity to adapt. By forces of constraint we mean, broadly speaking, environmental factors: geophysical configuration, climate, availability of land, food production and epidemic attacks. These constraining forces hinder that ideal demographic development which might be expected in a kind of Eden with unbounded food resources, limitless land, perfect climate and a total absence of hostile, pathogenic micro-organisms. It is possible to modify these constraints, but never quickly and never completely. Every community must come to terms with them, moulding and adapting its behaviour and, to some extent, its biological characteristics accordingly.

Scarcity of food is one of the chief obstacles, since it acts as a check on growth by boosting mortality or checking nuptiality along the lines of the Malthusian model discussed in the first chapter. The relationship of resources to survival is one of antagonism, mitigated, however, by the capacity of every demographic group to adapt both biologically and culturally. Cultural adaptation has manifested itself in a number of complex ways, sometimes passive but more often active, which entail with agricultural developments the production, exchange, preservation and preparation of food. Social and economic historians have dwelt at length on these types of adaptation. Less well known, however, are the mechanisms of biological adaptation which have enabled populations to survive nutritional stress over short, medium and even long periods. I have often referred to this adaptability during the course of this essay, but it is now time to give it wider consideration.

The human body has a remarkable ability to adapt to nutritional

111

stress through a number of mechanisms which vary according to the duration and character of the hardship or scarcity suffered. I have already discussed how a human being coping with short-term nutritional stress reacts by trying to re-establish an energetic equilibrium at a lower level, by burning fat reserves and expending less energy as a result of lower body weight, for a given level of physical activity. It is also to be noted that the basic metabolism seems to change more than proportionally in relation to weight, due to a more efficient consumption of the energy available. In more serious cases, reduced physical activity can further lower the threshold of caloric equilibrium.

This capacity to adapt over short periods is innate in the human species, forced to survive hundreds of thousands of years in unstable environments subject to sharp climatic variations. Mankind has developed a short-term strategy for dealing with temporary nutritional stress and minimising the harm that can be done by the vagaries of the weather, a poor harvest or even a whole year of failed harvests. It is a strategy whose time-span may be a month, a season or perhaps even a year. This flexibility has allowed the hunting and gathering Bushmen of the Kalahari to survive the dry season on 1,000 calories less than they can expect to consume in the good season.[1] For the Third World such swings in food availability are commonplace, as they were in many populations in the past.

There also exists a medium-term adaptability, which comes into operation in cases of prolonged nutritional stress and enables a population to develop a new equilibrium between food resources and reduced levels of consumption. This second line of defence entails reduced body growth in childhood and adolescence. Where stress is moderate, growth is slowed down while keeping a balance between height and weight. People whose growth is retarded in this fashion are not necessarily less efficient than others with normal growth.[2] The deviation of actual growth from the growth genetically possible under optimal food conditions (ignoring the negative influence of infections) can theoretically be split in two parts. One part is not connected with a heightened risk of infection and death, and is thus successfully adaptive; but over a certain threshold, which is difficult to determine, the risk of death increases, and this represents the non-adaptive part of the deviation. In the very long term, this non-adaptive lack of growth may also become genetically selective; but if so, its effects would not be discernible within the time-span familiar to demographers. A division of the two components of variation between actual height and theoretical height – one adaptive and the other not – is not possible for historical populations. However, in the medium to long term (a time-scale of decades or generations or, at most, centuries) a slowing down of skeletal and body growth such as occurred in some countries in the latter part of the eighteenth century would seem an efficient response to diminished food availability. This is a mechanism which tends to mitigate the negative effects that a slow erosion of food resources, provided these remain above a certain threshold, might otherwise have on survival. Thus, the human phenotype may assume body size compatible with the limits imposed by its environment. Growth is optimised relative to the resources available. It has been calculated, for instance, that stunting observed in many communities in less-developed countries can prevent an adult from attaining the normal weight of 70 kg., arresting it at 60 kg. Given the same amount of physical activity, this lower weight, together with a greater metabolic efficiency, would mean a 20 to 25 per cent saving of energy, 'a highly efficient strategy for survival, since the individual who had so adapted would avoid being caught in the well-known vicious circle of diminished physical activity'.[3] Indeed, diminished physical activity, while innocuous if temporary, does in the long run harm the economic and social efficiency of the individual and eventually leads to social regression. In a balanced environment, however, reduced body size would seem no disadvantage and in some environments appears to constitute an actual advantage.[4]

If we extrapolate on the basis of these conclusions from the individual to the community, we get an idea of the adaptive space of past populations. Where food was insufficient, a population could increase its chances of survival and maintain its demographic size at the expense of body weight. 'The adaptive strategy is to divide the supportable bio-mass among the largest number of persons, guaranteeing in so far as is possible the reproduction of future generations while simultaneously enhancing individual survivability through reduced demand.'[5] Lasker and Womack have thus summarised the greater saving of energy by the Mexican population as compared with that of the United States: with a population of 23.8 per cent of the US population (1970), the Mexican bio-mass was only 17.2 per cent of the American one and the proportion of fat only 14.7 per cent.[6] This kind of comparison between two modern populations can serve as a cautious guideline for the interpretation of historical cases and the evaluation of the consequences of a diversity of nutritional situations in different populations or in one population at different times.[7]

The reduction in height which occurred in some European populations during the latter part of the eighteenth century, in addition to being a symptom of impoverished nutrition, is also a sign that adaptation took the form of slowed body growth rather than increased mortality. On the other hand, the famine which afflicted a large part of the Russian population after the Revolution, while causing loss of weight and height in the growing generations, also led to increased mortality.[8] The violence of the shock was such that the defence mechanism failed.

Above a certain threshold, prolonged nutritional stress does not allow the adaptive process to avert the damage reflected in increased mortality. One can, however, imagine that a long history of want and deprivation might exercise a selective pressure in favour of those organisms which make the most efficient use of meagre food supplies. Authoritative opinion maintains that prolonged under-nourishment may result in the negative selection of children with greater growth potential who are more likely to perish. The small stature characterising populations which have suffered from a long history of food shortage may have a genetic explanation. This would account, for instance, for the lower stature of Meso-American populations.[9] This mechanism, however, acts only over the very long term; it is not adaptive in the sense in which we have so far used the expression, because it is connected with higher mortality.

The last type of adaptability is that which enables populations to absorb gradual changes in the composition of diets without this affecting their capacity for survival. One thinks, for example, of the capacity of the Eskimos to survive on a diet nine-tenths of whose caloric content is derived from animal foods; of the ability of certain African populations who lack salt to limit its loss in sweat and urine;[10] and of the vast range of diets consumed by contemporary populations, from those almost exclusively vegetarian to those over-rich in animal nutrients. We can presume that over the long term, populations have had no problem in adapting even to considerable changes of diet brought about by slow climatic changes or other factors. Damage occurs, however, in situations of rapid change when biological, or above all social, adaptability does not have sufficient time to come into operation.[11] For instance, the introduction and diffusion of maize, economically advantageous to peasant families, gave rise to pellagra, and sudden changes in diet due to migration may have caused other imbalances.[12]

It would be foolish to exaggerate the effects of the undoubted human capacity to adapt in the face of nutritional stress, but it is equally foolish to overlook its positive action. Once again, the biological and the social meet and merge in combinations and with consequences that are only partially distinguishable.

Nutrition and Malthusian repressive checks

It is useful at this point to reconsider the relationship between nutrition and mortality and to see to what extent the former – the 'subsistence' of Malthus and other classical economists – did indeed act as a check on demographic expansion. We should also try to determine whether the variations in mortality in the centuries leading up to the nineteenth were entirely or only partially attributable to the availability of food. The various lines of research pursued in the foregoing chapters do not provide us with a clear answer, but they do give an idea of whether the scales are tipped for or against the view that nutrition has been a major determinant in the course of mortality. I maintain that the scale pan containing elements contradicting the nutritional hypothesis – that nutrition is not a decisive factor in increased mortality – is weightier than the scale pan on which are balanced the elements in its favour. I shall try to summarise the elements that substantiate this view, dividing them into groups according to their logical affinity.

The first group of elements concerns the relationship between nutrition and susceptibility to infectious processes. This relationship does exist, but only at high levels of malnutrution. When caloric deficiency does not deviate much from the abstract ideal standard, the relationship seems not to operate. Or if it does, its effects are not felt since they are countered to varying degrees by the biological and social mechanisms of adaptability: physical activity is reduced; body growth slows down; less food is wasted and new sources of food are tapped. This capacity to adapt would seem to be demonstrated by the absence of any connection between fluctuations in grain prices and mortality, apart from those cases where an exceptional upsurge in prices indicates a severe famine. Moreover, there can be no doubt about the causal chain which links serious want and periods of high mortality: these are almost always the result of an epidemic attack – typhus is often clearly recognisable – triggered more by social dislocation than by malnutrition.

The second group of elements concerns the comparison between social classes and populations with ample food resources, such as élites and new countries, and communities for whom scarcity was the norm. In terms of survival, the former do not seem to have had a clear advantage over the latter. They also seem to be on a par as far as the decline in mortality in different age groups in periods of transition is concerned, and this includes the first year or first months of life when nutrition consists almost exclusively of maternal milk. The fact that infant mortality varied so much among preindustrial populations inclines one to believe that its level depended much more on environmental, cultural and social factors reflected in child-rearing methods than on nutritional factors which were uniform up to the age of weaning.

A third group of elements concerns nutritional trends from the end of the Middle Ages until the nineteenth century. The abundance of food resources, of meat especially, in the 100 or 150 years following the first outbreak of the plague, seems to coincide with a period of high mortality. In later centuries, cereal resources seem to have been by and large adequate, at least in normal years. An aspect not sufficiently stressed is the complementary role of home-production from direct domestic consumption by agricultural communities, particularly in less densely-populated areas. The widespread consumption of wine in vine-growing areas and of beer in northern countries is evidence of the existence of productive margins devoted to the cultivation of non-essential foodstuffs. The trends of real wages, in so far as these can tell us something about the changing standard of living among large sections of the population, seem, contrary to expectation, to be positively correlated with trends in mortality: wages are high when the death-rate is high at the end of the Middle Ages; they rise when the death-rate rises, both in England and elsewhere, in the seventeenth century; they fall when it falls at the end of the eighteenth century. The strong exogenous component of mortality constituted by infections and epidemics explains this lack of consistency between mortality and standard of living in the preindustrial age.

The observations made on the course of diets across time do not take into account – it must again be admitted – the variations in the distribution of food supplies or, to put it differently, the changing entitlement to food. A constant global level of food supply may conceal great variations of distribution, and so conceal varying proportions of the population living below the threshold of malnutrition. This fact can influence the mortality trends and, though difficult to quantify, should not be ignored.[13]

A final group of elements casts doubt on the association between the decline in mortality in the second half of the eighteenth century and the food situation. It is clear that there was a decline in the number of *ancien régime* crises and this fact in itself accounts for some of the improvement. But what is less clear is whether in 'normal' years there actually was an improvement in nutritional standards. In fact, proof abounds to the contrary. In France, where mortality was on the decline, nutritional standards showed no improvement and the same goes for other European countries. Height, a significant index of nutritional trends, decreased in many parts of Europe during the second half of the eighteenth century and so did real wages. The introduction and spread of new crops, such as the potato and maize, fed new mouths but did not improve the overall nutritional standard.

The other pan of the scale contains a number of facts that point to an undeniable connection between nutrition and mortality. Although the average caloric balance was certainly adequate in times of normality, its composition in terms of nutritional value may have been unbalanced and not the best guarantee for survival. Above all, we must remember the frequency of severe famines which in the sixteenth and seventeenth centuries, for instance, struck hard every twenty or thirty years. If it is true that the bursts of high mortality in years of famine were due more to epidemic factors connected with social disorganisation than to undernourishment – it must be remembered that it is only in orderly modern societies that starvation is the direct cause of a large number of deaths – the prime cause of this disorganisation is to be sought in the poverty of harvests and the scarcity of food. The disappearance, or at least mitigation, of these crises from the eighteenth century onwards, due to the introduction of new crops, the development and expansion of markets, and the spread of public relief schemes, removed one obstacle to demographic growth. The extent of this improvement is hard to evaluate because many epidemic crises disappeared (we need only think of the plague) or became attenuated for reasons independent of nutritional fluctuations. Moreover, explanatory models are in general rigid and mechanical and therefore of little assistance.

Let us suppose, however, that an *ancien régime* population was subject to a severe crisis every twenty-five years and that this caused a clear 4 per cent drop in the population[14] – both usual hypotheses for the period under discussion. Let us suppose also that the normal rate of increase of the population was four per thousand per year.[15] It is easy to calculate that after a century a population unaffected by crises would have increased by 49 per cent, while one affected by a crisis every quarter of a century would see its increase almost halved, to 27 per cent. Little would be gained by multiplying hypotheses.[16] The point is that mortality crisis provided a curbing element, even if only partially imputable to nutritional deficiency, and that its progressive weakening strengthened the forces of growth. On a more general level, Helleiner's comment on the elimination of that most frightening aspect of crises, the plague, merits mention: 'perhaps only a

Table 20 *Phases in nutrition and demography among European populations*

Variables	1350–1500	1500–1600	1600–1700	1700–1800	From 1800
Animal-based nutrition	Plentiful	Declining	Low	Low	Low point and recovery
Cereal-based nutrition	Plentiful	Adequate	Adequate	Adequate	Adequate
Standard of living (real wages)	Sharp improvement	Worsening	Worsening and recovery	Recovery and worsening	Recovery
Height	?	?	?	Increase and decrease	Increase and static
Famine and poverty	Frequent	Very frequent	Very frequent	Declining	Declining and cessation
New crops	–	Trials	Earl adoption	Adoption	Adoption
Demographic expansion	Negative, nil	Steady	None, slight	Slight, high	High
Mortality	Very high	Normal	High	Normal and declining	Declining
Incidence and severity of mortality crisis	Very high and severe	High and severe	High and severe	Declining	Declining

society freed from the fear as well as from the material and spiritual consequences of sudden death was able to achieve that high rate of intellectual and technical progress without which population growth could not have been sustained'.[17]

If, therefore, nutrition is absolved from the accusation of being the decisive element in mortality in normal years, it is at least partially guilty of having curbed growth through more or less frequent occurrences of shortage. The Malthusian repressive check from food shortage did not act over the long term but rather in short bursts. However, it should again be stressed that only a part, and not the main part, of the mortality crises of the past can be attributed to the nutritional factor; a larger part, with plague and smallpox in leading positions, had nothing to do with nutrition.

A return to Malthus by other routes

The Malthusian model discussed in the third section of the first chapter is now to be deprived of one of its principal tenets. The repressive check caused by a shortage of food does act, but only very weakly and almost exclusively in connection with severe famines. In Europe, periods of low demographic pressure have been characterised by a higher standard of living, by wages with greater purchasing power, and better quality food; but also by shrinking or stagnating populations and relatively high levels of mortality.[18] Periods of demographic expansion can be a direct result of lower mortality or, at least, of not higher than average mortality, but they are also accompanied by higher nutritional stress and lowered standards of living. This hardly agrees with the Malthusian model which postulates more or less the opposite. It does not agree because, as I have attempted to show, mortality seems largely independent of the availability of food resources. Why should this be so? The answer lies in the predominant role played by infectious and epidemic diseases in determining the level of mortality and because, as we have seen, the effect of those diseases was largely unrelated to the level of nutrition. The historical and epidemiological vicissitudes of the plague, typhus, smallpox and so many other diseases are far from fully understood. They were undoubtedly influenced by social and demographic factors, such as population density, urban expansion and mobility, all of which gradually brought about substantial changes in the spread of contagion and therefore of mortality. It has been proved that there are thresholds in population size and density below which certain infectious pathologies, such as smallpox, cannot survive. The effect of a disease lasting at epidemic level for any period of time is twofold: it increases the proportion of people immune to it and it also increases the normal death-rate. Conversely, when infection drops below epidemic level and the proportion of the population immunised falls, the population becomes susceptible should the infection be reintroduced from outside the community. The persistence or disappearance of a disease depends on its relative level of transmissibility.[19] This in turn depends partly upon the virulence of the pathogenic organisms, partly on the frequency of contact between carriers and sufferers (contagion) and partly on the immunological resistance of the person (dependent to some extent on his diet). The first two factors are probably more important than the last, and their fluctuation across time no doubt explains past variations in levels of contagion and mortality.

For these reasons, mortality appears to be a phenomenon by and large autonomous of the Malthusian system which links population and resources. The largely exogenous role of mortality does not negate the demographic relevance of the production and availability of food but, rather than being seen in terms of the nutrition–mortality relation, these act as a stimulus or check on nuptiality and the creation of households.

The demographic expansion of the thirteenth, sixteenth and eighteenth centuries took place against a background of great tension between population and food resources. Increasing demand was met with difficulty even when new lands were put under cultivation. When agricultural expansion was checked for institutional, political or geographic reasons, so was the multiplication of family units.[20] It is this mechanism which, when functioning, regulates growth in the Malthusian system. In fact, in cases of growing tension between population and resources it is unlikely that mortality will increase enough to re-establish an equilibrium, partly because the adaptation mechanism prevents the shortage of food from increasing the risk of death and partly because such increases were largely due to the epidemic factors I have postulated as being only very loosely connected with nutrition.

The availability of virgin land accompanied medieval demographic growth and the colonisation of eastern Europe.[21] A similar role was played by the tilling and reclaiming of land in many parts of sixteenth-century Europe, drainage and the creation of polders reached a zenith at the beginning of the seventeenth century.[22] Similarly, demographic growth in the eighteenth century was achieved as farming pushed back the frontiers of uncultivated land. In France, when the *ancien régime* was nearing its close, cultivated territory amounted to almost twenty-four million hectares as against the nineteen million of thirty years before.[23] In England, whereas enclosures at the beginning of the eighteenth century amounted to a few hundred acres, by the second half of the century they were increasing by 70,000 acres per year. The swamps and marshes of the Maremma and Prussia were drained as were the bogs and fens of Ireland, thus going some way towards satisfying the craving for land.[24] It is a process which permeated a large part of eighteenth-century Europe, and whose relation with demographic growth, differential timing, and mechanisms of cause and effect it would be interesting to explore.

But this is material for other research. I would like to conclude these pages with a phrase from Thomas Mann, who puts it in a nutshell: 'Life is an obstinate and indomitable cat, hard to kill, and so is mankind.'[25] Mankind who, by adapting, has withstood the clash with factors of constraint.

Notes

1 Demographic growth in Europe

1 A number of historians and demographers have attempted to quantify the evolution of the population of the world and of its various continents. Among the earlier ones I shall mention Beloch, Willcox and Carr-Saunders. Two good recent surveys are that by J. D. Durand, 'Historical Estimates of World Population: an Evaluation', *Population and Development Review*, 3 (1977), no. 3, pp. 253–96, and that by J. N. Biraben, 'Essai sur l'évolution du nombre des hommes', *Population*, 34 (1979) no. 1, pp. 13–25. A handy reference book is the compilation by C. McEvedy and R. Jones, *Atlas of World Population History* (London, Penguin, 1978).

2 A. E. Wrigley, 'The Growth of Population in Eighteenth-Century England: A Conundrum Resolved', *Past and Present*, 98 (1983).

3 In a stable population with constant birth and death-rates, the age structure and the rate of increase are also constant in time. This is expressed in the fundamental relation:

$$R_o = e^{rT}$$

where R_o is the net reproduction rate, or numbers of daughters per head that each generation of women brings into the world during the reproductive span. This can be expressed as:

$$R_o = \Sigma f_x l_x$$

where f_x denotes age-specific fertility rates, or number of girls born to each woman aged x; l_x denotes the survival function, namely the relationship between the survivors to age x and the number of births x years ago. In the first equation, T denotes the interval between generations corresponding roughly to the average age of child-bearing which in human populations varies within a fairly narrow range (27–33 years) depending on demographic pattern; and r denotes the rate of growth of the stable population. Thus, in this ideal stable population, the rate of growth, r, varies directly with R_o, the number of daughters per woman, and inversely with T. If R_o remains constant and T grows, r falls; and vice versa. It should be added that the net reproduction rate, R_o, is closely related to the gross reproduction rate, GRR, which is simply the sum of the f_x and expresses the number of daughters per woman in the hypothetical absence of death. The relationship between R_o and GRR is well approximated by $R_o=GRRl_a$, where l_a is the probability of surviving from birth to the average child-bearing age. Thus the first equation can be rewritten as:

$$Rl_a=e^{rT}$$

If T were fixed (in fact it is not, but the variations are small, as I said above), the rate of growth, r, could be expressed as a function of l_a, the index of mortality and GRR, the index of fertility. In addition, l_a is closely linked with e_o, the life expectancy at birth, which means that r can be expressed as a function of GRR and e_o. This is what is done, employing simplifications, in Figure 3.

4 R. M. May and D. Rubinstein, 'Reproduction Strategies' in C. R. Austin and R. V. Short (eds.), *Reproductive Fitness* (Cambridge, Cambridge University Press, 1986).

5 A. J. Coale, 'The Decline of Fertility in Europe since the Eighteenth Century as a Chapter of Human Demographic History' in A. J. Coale and S. C. Watkins (eds.), *The Decline of Fertility in Europe* (Princeton, Princeton University Press, 1986), p. 6.

6 A. Smith, *The Wealth of Nations* (London, Dent, 1964), vol. I, p. 71.

7 T. R. Malthus, *An Essay on the Principle of Population* (London, Penguin, 1979), pp. 70–1. Many other writers, well before Malthus, had already commented on the relationship between food resources and demographic growth. Schumpeter sees in Giovanni Botero a real precursor, antedating Malthus by 200 years. Already then Botero contrasted the strong capacity of population to increase with its weaker ability to grow food resources. Celibacy or devastation by war or disease restored the balance. See Schumpeter, *History of Economic Analysis* (New York, Oxford University Press, 1954), part II, chapter 5. Cantillon commented: 'Men multiply as Mice in a Barn if they have unlimited means of subsistence'; and Steuart:

Thus the generative faculty resembles a spring loaded with a weight, which always exerts itself in proportion to the diminution of resistance: when food has remained some time without augmentation or diminution, a generation will carry numbers as high as possible; if then food comes to be diminished, the spring is overpowered; the force of it becomes less than nothing. Inhabitants will diminish . . . If . . . food be increased . . . people will begin to be better fed; they will multiply and, in proportion as they increase in numbers, the food will become scarce again.

See R. Cantillon, *Essai sur la nature du commerce en général*, translated from the first French edition of 1755 by H. Riggs (London, Macmillan, 1931), p. 83; and J. Steuart, *An Inquiry into the Principles of Political Oeconomy*, ed. A. S. Skinner (Edinburgh and London, Oliver and Boyd, 1966), pp. 32–3.

8 D. Ricardo, *The Principles of Political Economy and Taxation* (London, Dent, 1965), p. 57.

9 The description of positive and preventive checks and their *modus operandi* is given in the first edition of Malthus' *Essay* (see note 7 above) in chapters 4 and 5, pp. 89–94. See also chapter 2 of the sixth edition (1826) of the *Essay* (London, Dent, 1967), vol. I, pp. 12–19 (being a reprint of the seventh edition, which is a definitive version of the 1826 edition). Another formu-

lation of the theory appears in the revised entry for 'Population' contributed by Malthus to the *Encyclopaedia Britannica* in 1824, and republished in 1830 under the title of 'A Summary View of the Population'; reprinted with his *Essay*, pp. 249–53.

10 E. A. Wrigley and R. S. Schofield, *The Population History of England, 1541–1871* (London, Arnold, 1981), chapter 11. See also H. J. Habakkuk, *Population Growth and Economic Development Since 1790* (Leicester, Leicester University Press, 1972).

11 P. Goubert, *Beauvais et les Beauvaisis de 1600 à 1730* (Paris, SEVPEN, 1920).

12 J. Dupâquier, *La population rurale du Bassin Parisien à l'époque de Louis XIV* (Paris, Ecole des Hautes Etudes en Sciences Sociales, 1979), pp. 371–91.

13 K. H. Connell, *The Population of Ireland 1750–1845* (Oxford, Clarendon Press, 1950). Since this publication, writers have continued to return to the subject, reinterpreting, correcting and criticising Connell's work, even though his arguments are accepted as well-founded in the main. M. Drake takes the opposite point of view in 'Marriage and Population Growth in Ireland, 1750–1845', *Economic History Review*, 2nd series, no. 16 (1963), as does L. M. Cullen in 'Irish History Without the Potato', *Past and Present*, July 1968, no. 40. In this context, see also J. Mokyr and C. O. Grada, 'New Developments in Irish Population History, 1700–1850', *The Economic History Review*, 37 (1984), no. 4, pp. 473–88.

14 E. Le Roy Ladurie, *Les paysans de Languedoc* (Paris, SEVPEN, 1969).

15 For Catalonia, see J. Nadal, 'La Població' in *Història de Catalunya*, ed. J. Nadal i Farreras and P. Wolff (Barcelona, Oikos-Tau, 1982). J. Nadal and E. Giralt, *La population Catalane de 1553 à 1717* (Paris, SEVPEN, 1961). For Provence, see R. Baehrel, *Une croissance: la Basse Provence rurale* (Paris, SEVPEN, 1961). For Italy, a Malthusian interpretation of fluctuations over a long period will be found in A. Bellettini, 'La popolazione italiana dall'inizio dell'era volgare ai giorni nostri. Valutazione e tendenze', *Storia d'Italia* (Turin, Einaudi, 1973), vol. V. See also M. A. Romani, *Nella spirale di una crisi* (Milan, Giuffrè, 1975).

16 T. K. Helleiner, 'The Population of Europe from the Black Death to the Eve of the Vital Revolution' in *The Economy of Expanding Europe in the Sixteenth and Seventeenth Centuries*, E. E. Rich and C. Wilson (eds.), *The Cambridge Economic History of Europe* (Cambridge, Cambridge University Press, 1967), vol. IV. C. M. Cipolla, 'Four Centuries of Italian Demographic Development' in D. V. Glass and D. E. C. Eversley (eds.), *Population in History* (London, Arnold, 1965).

17 T. McKeown, *The Modern Rise of Population* (London, Arnold, 1976), and by the same author, 'Food, Infection and Population', *Journal of Interdisciplinary History*, 14 (1983), no. 2, pp. 227–47.

18 V. G. Childe, *Man Makes Himself* (New York, Mentor, 1951).

19 M. N. Cohen and G. J. Armelagos, *Paleopathology and the Origin of Agriculture* (Orlando, Academic Press, 1984), pp. 1–7, 559–601.

20 Chapter five covers this area in greater depth. The main proponent of this thesis is W. Abel, *Congiuntura agraria e crisi agrarie* (Turin, Einaudi, 1976), pp. 104–7; see also L. White, *Mediaeval Technology and Social Change* (Oxford, Clarendon Press, 1962), where the author argues that the introduction in eighth-century Europe of triennial as opposed to biennial crop rotation boosted productivity considerably, stimulated the cultiva-

tion of new land and improved diet by allowing an expansion in the cultivation of protein-rich vegetables. 'Not only the greater amount of food produced by improved techniques, but also the type of nutrients produced contributed a great deal to explain, at least for northern Europe, the astonishing demographic expansion, the growth and proliferation of towns, the growth of industrial production, the extension of trade and exuberance of spirit which re-animated that age.' This thesis is even more extreme than McKeown's and, like all explanations which attribute to a single factor phenomena as complicated as demographic growth, is not very convincing.

2   *Energy, nutrition and survival*

1 For a sound analysis of the areas discussed in this chapter see A. E. and D. A. Bender, *Nutrition for Medical Students* (London, Wiley, 1982). See also E. S. Wing and A. B. Brown, *Paleonutrition* (New York, Academic Press, 1979); the National Academy of Sciences, *Recommended Daily Allowances* (Washington, 1980); and the World Health Organisation, *Energy and Protein Requirements*, the report of a joint FAO/WHO/UN expert consultation (Technical Report Series, no. 724, Geneva, 1985).

2 Bender and Bender, *Nutrition*, p. 22.

3 According to American standards, it is assumed that a recommended daily intake of 2σ above the mean will satisfy 97.5 per cent of the population, only 2.5 per cent having such elevated requirements as to need more calories. However, for the great majority of the population the recommended intake exceeds actual need. These are, therefore, 'prudential' standards that can be realistically applied to rich communities with ample material resources.

4 There can, of course, be exceptions to this in small communities struck by catastrophe, mass migration and so forth.

5 The average quantity of available calories in low-income developing countries barely exceeded this level at the beginning of the 1980s, and in some countries was actually below it. In India, for instance, the estimate for 1981 was 1,900 calories per head. See *World Development Report 1984* (Oxford, Oxford University Press, 1984), p. 265.

6 In the earlier part of this century, for instance, recommended protein consumption was much higher than it is nowadays.

7 Wing and Brown, *Paleonutrition*, p. 37. See also N. S. Scrimshaw and V. R. Young, 'The Requirements of Human Nutrition', *Scientific American*, September 1976.

8 Wing and Brown, *Paleonutrition*, p. 52.

9 See R. L. Wirsing, 'The Health of Traditional Societies and the Effects of Acculturation', *Current Anthropology*, 26 (1985), no. 3, pp. 303– 22.

10 J.-C. Toutain, 'La consommation alimentaire en France de 1789 à 1964', *Economie et Société*, Cahier de l'ISEA, vol. A, no. 11 (Geneva, 1971). ISTAT, *Statistiche storiche dell'Italia 1861–1975* (Rome, 1976).

11 This is the most commonly held opinion in historical studies of population. In particular, the decline in the death-rate in some European countries at the end of the eighteenth century is ascribed to an improvement in diet. As we saw in chapter one, there is a tendency for

McKeown's position in this field to go unchallenged, with the result that nutritional changes are often taken as an adequate explanation for changes in mortality.

12 This is a very wide sector of the biomedical sciences and the layman may have trouble finding his way around it. See R. K. Chandra and P. M. Newberne, *Nutrition, Immunity and Infection* (New York, Plenum Press, 1977); R. N. Poston, 'Nutrition and Immunity' in R. J. Jarret (ed.), *Nutrition and Disease* (Baltimore, University Park Press, 1979); W. R. Beisel, 'Nutrition, Infection, Specific Immune Responses and Nonspecific Host Defences: a Complex Interaction' in R. R. Watson (ed.), *Nutrition, Disease Resistance and Immune Function* (New York, Marcel Dekker, 1984).

13 N. S. Scrimshaw, C. E. Taylor and J. E. Gordon, *Interaction of Nutrition and Infection*, Monograph Series no. 57 (Geneva, WHO, 1968). See also C. E. Taylor and C. de Sweemer, 'Nutrition and Infection' in M. Rechcigl (ed.), *Food, Nutrition and Health* (Basel, Karger, 1979), pp. 203–25.

14 R. Martorell and T. J. Ho, 'Malnutrition, Morbidity and Mortality' in H. Mosley and L. Chen (eds.), *Child Survival: Strategies for Research*, supplement to vol. 10 of *Population and Development Review*, 1984, p. 63.

15 Bender and Bender, *Nutrition*, pp. 26–7. Of course, adequacy of diet can be assessed using other measures, ranging from caloric budgets to clinical, chemical and biochemical analyses. However, these are difficult to obtain in mass surveys.

16 On this subject see A. A. Kielman and C. McCord, 'Weight for Age as an Index of Risk of Death in Children', *The Lancet*, 10 June 1978, pp. 1247–50; L. C. Chen, A. Chowdhury and S. L. Huffman, 'Anthropometric Assessment of Energy–Protein Malnutrition and Subsequent Risk of Mortality Among Pre-School Aged Children', *American Journal of Clinical Nutrition*, 33 (1980), pp. 1836–45; P. L. Trowbridge and A. Sommer, 'Nutritional Anthropometry and Mortality Risk', *American Journal of Clinical Nutrition*, 34 (1981), pp. 2591–2.

17 Scrimshaw, Taylor and Gordon, *Interaction*, p. 58.

18 R. Martorell and C. Yarbrough, 'The Energy Cost of Diarrheal Diseases and Other Common Illnesses in Children' in L. C. Chen and N. S. Scrimshaw (eds.), *Diarrhea and Malnutrition* (New York, Plenum Press, 1983). See also R. Martorell and J.-P. Habicht, 'Growth in Early Childhood in Developing Countries' in F. Falkner and J. M. Tanner (eds.), *Human Growth* (New York, Plenum Press, 1986), vol. III, pp. 251–2.

19 Poston, 'Nutrition', pp. 192–4. See also W. G. Bailey, *Human Longevity from Antiquity to the Modern Lab* (London, 1987). This is an annotated bibliography. Note the numerous titles devoted to the impact of experimental caloric reduction on animal survival.

20 A. Keys, J. Brozek, A. Henschel, O. Mikelsen and H. L. Taylor, *The Biology of Human Starvation* (Minneapolis, The University of Minnesota Press, 1950), vol. II, p. 1007.

21 Martorell and Ho, 'Malnutrition', p. 54.

22 *Ibid.*

23 Beisel, 'Nutrition, Infection', pp. 22–3; Chandra and Newberne, *Nutrition, Immunity*, pp. 7–8.

24 Poston, 'Nutrition', p. 194.

25 'Marasmus' comes from the Greek 'Marasmos', 'consumption', 'wasting

away'; 'Kwashiorkor' from the Ga language of Ghana, meaning 'laid-aside baby', that is a baby that is taken from the maternal breast to make way for a new-born baby, and is therefore deprived of mother's milk. These two diseases, widespread in tropical Africa and elsewhere, are cited among the consequences of 'proteic-caloric' malnutrition which are defined as a 'series of pathological conditions which derive from a simultaneous lack, to varying degrees, of proteins and calories, being very common in early infancy and children and associated very often with infective processes', see *FAO–WHO Expert Committee on Nutrition, Eighth Report,* WHO Reports, no. 471, Geneva, 1971, p. 1.

26 Poston, 'Nutrition', p. 194.
27 Keys *et al., The Biology,* p. 1010.
28 *Ibid.*
29 Chandra and Newberne, *Nutrition, Immunity,* p. 9.

3 *Famine and want*

1 V. R. Young and N. S. Scrimshaw, 'The Physiology of Starvation', *Scientific American,* October 1971.
2 E. S. Wing and A. B. Brown, *Paleonutrition* (New York, Academic Press, 1979), pp. 171–2.
3 I. Somis, *Ragionamento sopra il fatto avvenuto in Bergemoletto in cui tre donne, sepolte vive fra le rovine della stalla per la caduta di una gran mole di neve, sono state trovate vive dopo trentasette giorni [Discourse on the occurrence at Bergemoletto where three women, buried alive under the ruins of a cowshed after a great mass of snow had fallen, were found alive after thirty-seven days]* (Turin, Stampa Reale, 1758).
4 Young and Scrimshaw, 'The Physiology', p. 44.
5 K. Kelley, *The Longest Way. Northern Ireland and the IRA* (Dingle, Brandon Books, 1982).
6 A. Keys *et al., The Biology of Human Starvation* (Minneapolis, The University of Minnesota Press, 1950), vol. II, p. 1010. See also H. L. Taylor and A. Keys, 'Adaptation to Caloric Restriction', *Science,* 112, 25 August 1950, pp. 215–18.
7 Taylor and Keys, 'Adaptation', p. 215.
8 Keys *et al., The Biology,* pp. 1012–13.
9 F. Viteri and O. Pineda, 'Effect on Body Composition and Body Function', in G. Blix, Y. Hofvander and B. Vahlquist (eds.), *Famine: A Symposium dealing with Nutrition and Relief Operation in Times of Disaster* (Uppsala, Almquist and Wiksell, 1971), pp. 25–40. Other historically important studies are those by Benedict and his collaborators. See F. G. Benedict, *A Study of Prolonged Fasting* (Carnegie Institute, Washington Publ. no. 280, 1919). See also G. Lusk, 'The Physiological Effects of Undernutrition', *Physiological Reviews,* 1 (1921), no. 1, pp. 54–65; and S. Margulis, 'Fast and Famine', *The Scientific Monthly,* 16 (1923), no. 1, pp. 54–65.
10 Reale Commissione d'inchiesta sulle violazioni del diritto delle genti commesse dal nemico, *L'occupazione delle provincie invase* [The occupation of the invaded provinces], vol. 4 (Rome, Bestetti e Tumminelli, 1920–1). G. Mortara, *La salute pubblica degli Italiani durante e dopo la guerra* (Bari, Laterza, 1925), pp. 61–106.

11 Mortara, *La salute*.
12 Z. Stein, M. Susser, G. Saenger and F. Marolla, *Famine and Human Development* (New York, Oxford University Press, 1975), pp. 39–53.
13 M. Winick (ed.), *Hunger Disease* (New York, Wiley, 1979).
14 For instance, widespread starvation among Soviet rural populations between 1921 and 1923 claimed some millions of lives (five million according to one estimate). S. G. Wheatcroft, 'Soviet Famine and Food Supply Problems before the Second World War', *Famine in History Newsletter* (1981), no. 3. For descriptions of the pathology of the frequent outbursts of famine during the First World War, see M. M. Maver, 'Nutritional Edema and War Dropsy', *The Journal of the American Medical Association*, 74 (1920), April, pp. 934–41.
15 Keys *et al.*, *The Biology*, p. 1010.
16 *Ibid.*
17 *Ibid.*
18 W. H. Foege, 'Famine, Infections and Epidemics' in Blix *et al.* (eds.), *Famine*, pp. 65–7.
19 And most probably from many other, perhaps remoter, cases. According to Post, the high death-rate in various parts of Switzerland following the last great European subsistence crisis (1816–18) was a direct result of famine, as there were few incidents of an epidemic nature. J. Post, *The Last Great Subsistence Crisis in Western History* (Baltimore, Johns Hopkins University Press, 1977), p. 129.
20 See various contributions in Blix *et al.*, *Famine*.
21 A. Ferro-Luzzi, 'Range of Variation in Energy Expenditure and Scope for Regulation' in *Proceedings of the XIII International Congress of Nutrition* (Brighton, 1985), pp. 393–9.
22 G. Pinto, *Il libro del biadaiolo. Carestia e annona a Firenze dalla metà del '200 al 1348* (Florence, Olschki, 1978), p. 313.
23 J. Meuvret, 'Les crises de subsistence et la démographie de la France de l'Ancien régime', *Population*, 1 (1946), no. 4, pp. 643–50.
24 The literature on this subject is so extensive that to quote from it even schematically lies beyond the scope of this book. The works cited in this section have been reduced to the bare minimum and the reader is referred to a fuller bibliography for them.
25 F. Braudel, *Civilization matérielle, économie et capitalisme, XVème–XVIIIème siècles, vol. I: Les structures du quotidien; le possible et l'impossible* (Paris, Colin, 1979), p. 102.
26 Even a cursory look through Corradi will give a good picture of the great famines. A. Corradi, *Annali delle epidemie occorse in Italia dalle prime memorie fino al 1850* (Bologna, Forni, 1973) (reprint of original Bologna edition, 1865–94).
27 G. B. Segni, *Trattato sopra la carestia e fame, sue cause, accidenti, previsioni e reggimenti* (Bologna, Eredi di Giovanni Rossi, 1602), p. 54.
28 W. R. Aykroyd, 'Definition of different degrees of starvation' in Blix *et al.* (eds.), *Famine*, pp. 18–19.
29 Quoted by W. P. MacArthur, 'Medical History of the Famine' in R. D. Edwards and T. D. Williams (eds.), *The Great Famine* (New York, New York University Press, 1957), p. 257. The whole of MacArthur's essay

sheds much light on the mechanics of the bio-social fluctuations that linked famine with mortality in Ireland.

30 The belief that a weakening of the organism is the prime cause of a rise in mortality is still very much in vogue among historians and demographers who have not gone into the question in depth. Some authorities, however, have argued against this. Chambers, for instance, maintains that famines were not always accompanied by epidemic outbreaks, since such outbreaks were more often brought about by social upheaval than by malnutrition. When there was no epidemic, famine did not lead to a noticeable increase in mortality, but simply aggravated certain causes of death directly associated with nutrition, such as pneumonia and tuberculosis. See J. D. Chambers, *Population, Economy and Society in Pre-Industrial England* (London, Oxford University Press, 1972), pp. 87–8.

31 I. Kershaw, 'The Great Famine and Agrarian Crisis in England', *Past and Present*, 59, May 1973, pp. 3–50.

32 An excellent survey for England is given by A. B. Appleby in 'Grain Prices and Subsistence Crises in England and France, 1590–1790', *The Journal of Economic History*, 39 (1979), no. 4, pp. 865–87. See also by the same author, 'Disease or Famine? Mortality in Cumberland and Westmoreland, 1580–1640', *The Economic History Review*, 26 (1973), no. 7, pp. 403–32; and *Famine in Tudor and Stuart England* (Stanford, Stanford University Press, 1978); R. Schofield, 'The Impact of Scarcity and Plenty on Population Change in England, 1541–1871', *Journal of Interdisciplinary History*, 14 (1983), no. 2, pp. 265–91.

33 Chambers, *Population*, p. 92.

34 E. A. Wrigley and R. S. Schofield, *The Population History of England 1541–1871* (London, Arnold, 1981), p. 341.

35 For France the amount of material is truly enormous. See F. Lebrun's summary, 'Les crises de démographie en France aux XVIIème et XVIIIème siècles', *Annales ESC*, 35 (1980), no. 2, pp. 205–33. Other fundamental works besides Meuvret's article are P. Goubert, *Beauvais et les Beauvaisis de 1600 à 1730* (Paris, SEVPEN, 1920), and F. Lebrun, *Les hommes et la mort en Anjou aux XVIIème et XVIIIème siècles* (Paris, Mouton, 1971).

36 F. Lebrun, 'Les crises', p. 220.

37 W. Abel, *Massenarmut und Hungerkrisen im Vorindustriellen Europa* (Hamburg, Paul Parey, 1974).

38 E. F. Heckscher, *An Economic History of Sweden* (Cambridge, Mass., Harvard University Press, 1954), p. 137.

39 G. Parenti, *Prime ricerche sulla rivoluzione dei prezzi in Firenze* (Florence, 1939); and by the same author, *Prezzi e mercato a Siena (1546–1765)* (Florence, 1942). Both works have been reprinted in G. Parenti, *Studi di storia dei prezzi* (Paris, Maison des Sciences de l'Homme, 1981).

40 L. Del Panta, 'Cronologia e diffusione delle crisi di mortalità in Toscana dalla fine del XIV secolo agli inizi del XIX secolo', *Ricerche Storiche*, 7 (1977), no. 2, pp. 293–343.

41 A. Bellettini, 'Ricerche sulle crisi demografiche del seicento', *Società e Storia*, 1 (1978), no. 1, pp. 35–64.

42 Post, *The Last Great Subsistence Crisis*.

43 G. Felloni, 'Prezzi e popolazione in Italia nei secoli XVI–XIX' in Comitato

Italiano per lo Studio della Demografia Storica, *Demografia storica e condizioni economico–sociali* (Rome, CISP, 1976), pp. 100–2.
44 V. Perez Moreda, *Las crisis de mortalidad en la España interior, siglos XVI–XIX* (Madrid, Siglo Veinteuno, 1980).
45 Perez Moreda, *Las crisis*, pp. 254–6 and 313.
46 In cases where a rise in mortality precedes a rise in prices there may operate a relation according to which the diffusion of disease, and the subsequent mortality, is the cause of the rise in prices (due to a shortage of workers for cultivation, harvest and transportation). Such, at least, is the direction of causality for the Spanish crisis of 1786–90. See V. Perez Moreda, 'Hambre, mortalidad y crecimiento demografico en las poblaciones de la Europa preindustrial', *Revista de Historia Económica*, 6 (1988), no. 3. I cite this work also because it contains an interesting discussion of the Spanish edition of this book: in this English edition I take into account some of Moreda's points of criticism.
47 G. Da Molin, 'Carestia ed epidemia del 1763–64 in Capitanata', *Rivista di Storia dell'Agricoltura*, 18 (1978), no. 1, pp. 69–108.
48 R. Lee, 'Short-Term Variations: Vital Rates, Prices and Weather'; ninth chapter in Wrigley and Schofield, *The Population History of England*, pp. 356–401, particularly pp. 356–9 and 372–84.
49 Lee, 'Short-Term Variations', p. 378.
50 D. R. Weir, 'Life under Pressure: France and England, 1670–1870', *Journal of Economic History*, 44 (1984), no. 1, pp. 27–47.
51 For this period, however, the death series excludes those under the age of five.
52 See chapter five.
53 See the source of Table 11.
54 Chambers, *Population*, p. 92.
55 T. Bengtsson and R. Ohlsson, 'Age Specific Mortality and Short-Term Changes in the Standard of Living: Sweden 1751–1859', *European Journal of Population*, 1 (1985), no. 3, pp. 309–26.
56 B. H. Slicher Van Bath, *Storia agraria dell'Europa Occidentale (1500–1850)* (Turin, Einaudi, 1972), pp. 164–5.
57 Parenti, *Prezzi*, p. 197.
58 I refer the reader to C. M. Cipolla's wise words in *Contro un nemico invisibile* (Bologna, Il Mulino, 1985), pp. 38–9.
59 This is a simplification of what were in fact much more complex upheavals. Famine probably led to a very serious impoverishment in the diet of a fairly large part of the population which already lived at subsistence level. My argument has been developed without reference to the access to food or how this varies over time. More research on this topic is indispensable to the progress of historical–demographic analysis. An illuminating study in this regard which deals with modern famines in developing countries is A. Sen's *Poverty and Famines* (Oxford, Clarendon Press, 1981). According to Sen, modern famines have less to do with a fall in food production, and therefore in total global resources, than with variations in the 'right of access' to food, changes which are harmful to a greater or smaller part of the population.

4 *The starving and the well-fed*

1 M. Neveux, 'L'alimentation du XIVème au XVIIIème siècles', *Revue d'Histoire Economique et Sociale*, 3 (1973), p. 377.

2 Neveux, 'L'alimentation', pp. 377–8.

3 T. H. Hollingsworth, 'Mortality in the British Peerage Families since 1600', *Population*, 32 (1977), pp. 323–52.

4 During the course of this chapter I shall often refer to values taken from life tables. It seems appropriate to define some of these for the benefit of readers unfamiliar with them. A life table expresses the gradual extinction, with increase in age, of a group of newborns, initially composed (by convention) of 10^n individuals, say 1,000. The values l_x, where x denotes age, represent the survivors from the initial 1,000 on each successive birthday until the complete extinction of the generation. Another fundamental function of the table, to which I shall often refer, is q_x and represents the probability (expressed by convention per 1,000 or another power of 10) which the survivors to age x have of dying before birthday $x+1$. These probabilities can also be applied to a period longer than a year, and the prefix 1 or 4 or 5 indicates the number of years to which this probability applies. Thus, in Table 14, $_1q_0$ indicates the probability that a generation of newborns, l_0, has of dying before first birthday; $_4q_1$ indicates the probability that those surviving to their first birthday, l_1, will die before their fifth; $_5q_5$ indicates the probability that those surviving to their fifth birthday, l_5, will die before their tenth, and so on.

   Finally, another frequently used function is life expectancy, e_x (x referring to a specific age), which indicates the additional years that the survivors to age x, l_x, can on average expect to live according to the mortality levels given in the table. This is obtained by calculating the number of years to be lived by the generation after birthday x and dividing by the number of survivors at age x, l_x. The value e_0 expresses 'life expectancy at birth'. Here an apparent paradox should be noted: in life tables that reflect the high mortality typical of traditional demographic regimes, life expectancy rises during the first few years of life (e_0, e_1, ... e_5) and sometimes even beyond. This occurs because during the first years of life many individuals are eliminated who therefore contribute little to the total sum of years which the generation as a whole has still to live. This in turn depresses the average value of life expectancy. When, after a few years, this effect wears out, life expectancy begins to decline with the increase of age. One should keep in mind, however, that in a high mortality regime, the value of e_{20}, for example, can still be greater than that of e_0.

5 E. A. Wrigley and R. S. Schofield, *The Population History of England, 1541–1871* (London, Arnold, 1981), p. 230.

6 T. H. Hollingsworth, 'A Note on the Medieval Longevity of the Secular Peerage', *Population Studies*, 29 (1977), no. 1, p. 157. It has been argued that the relatively high mortality of peers and other privileged groups could be attributed to gastronomic excesses; but I am inclined to doubt this since women who may be said to be more abstemious were also prone to high mortality.

7 T. H. Hollingsworth, 'A Demographic Study of the British Ducal Families', *Population Studies*, 11 (1957), no. 1, pp. 4–26.

8 J. C. Russell, *British Medieval Population* (Albuquerque, University of New Mexico Press, 1948), p. 186.

9 S. Peller, 'Births and Deaths among Europe's Ruling Families since 1500' in D. V. Glass and D. E. Eversley (eds.), *Population in History* (London, Arnold, 1965).

10 J. Houdaille, 'Mortalité masculine dans les familles regnantes au Moyen Age', *Population*, 27 (1972), no. 6, pp. 1131–3.

11 Hollingsworth, 'A Note on the Medieval Longevity', pp. 157–8.

12 L. Henry, *Anciennes familles Genevoises* (Paris, INED, 1956).

13 M. Livi-Bacci, 'Ebrei, aristocratici e cittadini: precursori del declino della fecondità', *Quaderni storici*, 28 (1983), pp. 913–39.

14 A. Perrenoud, 'L'inégalité sociale devant la mort à Genève au XVIIIème siècle', *Population*, 30 (1975), special number, p. 239.

15 P. R. Galloway, *Population, Prices and Weather in Preindustrial Europe*, unpubl. thesis (Berkeley, University of California, 1987), p. 228.

16 I refer the reader to note 4. According to Coale and Demeny's tables, for instance, in the 'West' model the life expectancy for males at age 20 was 29.3 years, as against 22.9 years at age 0, and so forth for other pairs of values: 30.6 against 25.3; 31.8 against 27.7; 33.1 against 30.1; 34.3 against 32.5.

17 L. Henry and C. Levy, 'Ducs et Pairs sous l'Ancien Régime: caractéristiques démographiques d'une caste', *Population*, 15 (1960), no. 5.

18 S. Salvini, *La mortalità dei Gesuiti in Italia nei secoli XVI e XVII* (Firenze, Dipartimento Statistico, 1979).

19 J. Hatcher, 'Mortality in the Fifteenth Century: Some New Evidence', *Economic History Review*, 2nd series, 39 (1986), no. 1, pp. 19–38.

20 H. Le Bras and D. Dinet, 'Mortalité des laïques et mortalité des religieux: les Bénédectins de Saint Maur aux XVII et XVIII siècles', *Population*, 13 (1980), no. 2, p. 356.

21 J. Graunt, 'Natural and Political Observations upon the Bills of Mortality' in C. H. Hull (ed.), *The Economic Writings of Sir William Petty* (New York, Kelley, 1964 reprint), vol. II, pp. 352–3.

22 See also R. V. Wells, *Revolutions in Americans' Lives* (Westport, Conn., Greenwood Press, 1982), p. 25. By the early nineteenth century the beneficial effects of plentiful food resources on demographic growth were widely noted: 'The English in the colonies will become more numerous in proportion in three generations than they would be in thirty in England, because in the Colonies they find for cultivation new tracts of land from which they drive the Savages' as R. Cantillon observes in *Essai sur la nature du commerce en général*, 1st French edn. 1755, English transl. by H. Higgs (London, Macmillan, 1931), p. 83.

23 H. Charbonneau, *Vie et mort de nos ancêtres* (Montreal, Les Presses de l'Université de Montreal, 1975), pp. 125 and 147.

24 R. Haines and R. O. Avery, 'The American Life Table of 1830–60: an Evaluation', *Journal of Interdisciplinary History*, 11 (1980), pp. 85–6. Fogel, starting from a sample of genealogies, reaches estimates of mortality noticeably lower than those relating to England for the whole of the eighteenth and nineteenth centuries. These estimates, however, are not very convincing for at least two reasons. The first is the small number of observations (barely 4,210 cases for the two centuries under considera-

tion). The second, more serious one, is that his sources consisted of printed biographical family genealogies, distorted in terms of geographical distribution, wealth and other characteristics, and doubtless incomplete due to the omission of the deaths of some members, especially those dying in the early years of life. Furthermore these genealogies, being mostly derived from reconstructions *ex post facto* of family trees or hearsay from the recollections of living members of the families, do not include the branches without issue, extinct at earlier stages. All this leads one to expect an underestimation of mortality. See R. W. Fogel, 'Nutrition and the Decline in Mortality since 1700: Some Additional Preliminary Findings', *NBER Working Paper Series No. 1802* (Cambridge, Mass., 1986), pp. 14–25, 43. Based on data for Massachusetts and Maryland, Jacobson arrives at an estimate for the entire United States in 1850 of 40.4 years for men and 42.9 for women. See P. H. Jacobson, 'An Estimate of the Expectation of Life in the United States in 1850', *Milbank Memorial Fund Quarterly*, 35 (1957), no. 2, pp. 197–201. This estimate is also accepted by A. J. Coale and M. Zelnick in *New Estimates of Fertility and Population in the United States, 1850–1968* (Princeton, Princeton University Press, 1973), pp. 8–9, who note the similarity of these figures to estimates for six European populations of the same period. For an assessment of historical tendencies in mortality prior to the mid-nineteenth century, see M. A. Vinovskis, 'Mortality Rates and Trends in Massachusetts before 1860', *Journal of Economic History*, 32 (1972), no. 1, pp. 184–213.

25 C. Darwin, *The Voyage of the Beagle* (London, Dent, 1959), p. 111.

26 The data for Buenos Aires are taken from M. S. Muller, 'Mortalidad en la Ciudad de Buenos Aires desde mediados del siglo XIX', in *Conferencia Regional Latino Americana de Población, Actas* (Mexico, El Colegio di Mexico, 1972), vol. 1, pp. 66–73. The estimates for Argentina, made by J. Somoza, are published in N. Sanchez Albornoz, *La Población de America Latina desde los tiempos precolombinos al año 2000* (Madrid, Alianza Universal, 1977), p. 191.

27 L. Henry and A. Pilatti Balhana, 'La population du Paranà depuis le XVIIIème siècle', *Population*, 30 (1975), special number, p. 184.

28 In Costa Rica, e_0 for both sexes was put at 25.9 for 1860, 27.6 for 1870, 28.6 for 1880, 30.1 for 1890, 31.6 for 1900. In Brazil, e_0 between 1870 and 1900 lay between 27.3 and 29.4; in Chile in 1900 it was estimated at 28.7. In other Latin American countries estimates, where they exist, show very low life expectancy at birth, below twenty-five years. But these countries can hardly be said to have enjoyed a thriving dietary situation. See E. Arriaga, *New Life Tables for Latin American Populations in the Nineteenth and the Twentieth Century*, Population Monograph Series, no. 3 (Berkeley, University of California, 1968).

29 Official Spanish tables show a level of e_0 at 29.1 in 1861–70 and 28.9 in 1877–87. Our estimates, based on the 1797 census and assuming stability, give a value of 26.8 at the end of the eighteenth century. Thus a slight increase may have taken place over the two centuries. See M. Livi-Bacci, 'Fertility and Nuptial Changes in Spain from the Late Eighteenth to the Early Twentieth Century', part 1, *Population Studies*, 22 (1968), no. 1, pp. 90–2. In Italy, the levels of life expectancy lay at around thirty-three years in the post-Unification period and may have been due to an

improvement in living conditions over the previous century. Any improvement there may have been, however, certainly pales by comparison with those recorded for the four countries in Table 12, where e_o reached, or even exceeded, a stable level of forty years by the mid-nineteenth century.

30 See, for example, the Swedish case for which there exists some data on the causes of death before the mid-nineteenth century: see G. Fridlizius, 'The Mortality Decline in the First Phase of the Demographic Transition: Swedish Experiences', in T. Bengtsson, G. Fridlizius and R. Ohlsson (eds.), *Pre-Industrial Population Change* (Stockholm, Almquist and Wiksell, 1984), p. 81.

31 Even though percentage variations in mortality are on average lower for age nought, the absolute variation is higher than at later ages, given the higher level of mortality. It will be noted that, taking the average across these four countries, the probability of death between age nought and age one is about equal to the probability of death between age one and age ten.

32 For example, in some areas of Bavaria. See J. Knodel and E. Van de Walle, 'Breastfeeding, Fertility and Infant Mortality: an Analysis of Some Early German Data', *Population Studies*, 22 (1968), no. 2.

33 C. A. Corsini, 'Structural Change in Infant Mortality in Tuscany from the Eighteenth to the Nineteenth Century' in Bengtsson *et al.* (eds.), *Pre-Industrial Population Change*, pp. 127–50.

34 According to INED (Institut National d'Etudes Démographiques) estimates, the value of e_o for France in the period under consideration was 28.7, and that of e_1 was 38.6. A drop in infant mortality from the French level of $q_o=273$ to the English level of $q_o=165$, holding mortality at later ages unchanged (at the French level), would have meant an increase of e_o from 27.7 to 33.1. The hypothesis of invariant mortality leads is unrealistic, since in practice mortality in the first year and mortality in later years cannot be totally independent of each other.

35 For example, in Geneva where there was a high mortality differential (see note 14 above) the decline in mortality followed a similar rhythm and pattern (according to age, for instance) across all social classes. This suggests that causes other than an improvement in dietary conditions were at work since food had been in ample supply for all for some time. See A. Perrenoud, 'Mortality Decline in its Secular Setting', in Bengtsson *et al.* (eds.), *Pre-Industrial Population Change*, pp. 41–69.

36 J. Houdaille, 'La mortalité des enfants dans la France rurale de 1690 à 1779', *Population*, 39 (1984), no. 1, p. 86.

37 E. A. Wrigley and R. S. Schofield, 'English Population History from Family Reconstitutions: Summary Results 1600–1799', *Population Studies*, 37 (1983), no. 2, p. 179.

38 O. Turpeinen, 'Infectious Diseases and Regional Differences in Finnish Death Rates 1749–73', *Population Studies*, 32 (1978), no. 3. For the purposes of research, Scania, the most densely populated southern region of Sweden, was divided into eight areas. In these it was found that during the decade 1781–90 infant mortality varied between a minimum of 193 and a maximum of 280 per thousand, and this in an area which was really quite homogeneous; see Fridlizius, 'The Mortality Decline', p. 76.

39 During the first half of the nineteenth century there were considerable

differences between Wallonia with low infant mortality and western Flanders with high infant mortality. See M. Poulain and D. Tabutin, 'La mortalité aux jeunes âges en Europe et en Amérique du Nord du XIXème à nos jours', in M. Boulanger and S. Tabutin (eds.), *La mortalité des enfants dans le monde et dans l'histoire* (Liège, Ordina, 1980), p. 135.

40 Unfortunately the studies relating to the eighteenth century tend neither to be very systematic nor to consider large enough areas. Yet certain marked differences do emerge between areas. For instance, in rural areas of the Veneto infant mortality was over 300 per thousand, whereas in rural Tuscany it was only 200. See L. Del Panta and M. Livi-Bacci, 'Le componenti naturali dell'evoluzione demografica', in Società Italiana di Demografia Storica, *La popolazione italiana nel Settecento* (Bologna, CLUEB, 1980), pp. 102–3.

41 See note 34 above.

42 While breast-feeding is, of course, a form of nutrition, we refer here to the nutrition derived from the products of agriculture, cattle breeding and fishing, whether self-produced or bought on the market. Such nutrition is tied to climatic, economic and other fluctuations, whereas breast-feeding is independent of these factors.

43 'Breastfeeding, Fertility and Family Planning', *Population Reports*, series J, no. 24 (1981), p. J528.

44 'Breastfeeding', p. J528.

45 O. Benedictow, 'The Milky Way in History: Breast-Feeding, Antagonism between the Sexes and Infant Mortality in Medieval Norway', *Scandinavian Journal of History*, 10 (1985), no. 1, pp. 28–9.

46 O. Ferrari, *De Arte Medica Infantium* (Brixiae, 1577), p. 45. Or, in the original Latin, *Lac enim eo in tempore indigesitible, crassum et vitiosum est, quod Latini vocant colostrum.*

47 N. Latronico, *Storia della pediatria* (Turin, Edizione Minerva Medica, 1977), pp. 256–7. See p. 269 of this work for Linnaeus' opinion on the beneficial effects of colostrum and breast-feeding in general. N. Rosen de Rosenstein, *Trattato delle malattie dei bambini transportato dal tedesco con alcune note di G. B. Palletta* (Milan, Monastero di S. Ambrogio Maggiore, 1783). R. Thomas, *Trattato delle malattie della gravidanza e del puerperio e delle malattie dei bambini*, 2nd transl. of an eighteenth-century work (Naples, 1828).

48 V. A. Fildes, *Breasts, Bottles and Babies* (Edinburgh, Edinburgh University Press, 1986), p. 86.

49 Corsini, 'Structural Change in Infant Mortality', pp. 130–2.

50 V. A. Fildes, *Breasts*, p. 91.

51 The literature on the nutritional value and immunological properties of breast-feeding is vast. See D. and E. Jelliffe, *Human Milk in the Modern World* (Oxford, Oxford University Press, 1978); R. N. Poston, 'Nutrition and Immunity' in R. J. Jarret (ed.), *Nutrition and Disease* (Baltimore, University Park Press, 1979), pp. 187 and 194; see also the substantial bibliography in 'Breastfeeding, Fertility and Family Planning'.

52 Benedictow in his study, 'The Milky Way', argues that the custom adopted in early eighteenth-century England of breast-feeding babies immediately after birth led to a sharp drop in mortality and that the reverse occurred in Norway in the early Middle Ages when it became the practice to delay breast-feeding. In the case of Finland, Turpeinen finds that, while between the eighteenth and nineteenth centuries the mortality rates for

later age groups remained unchanged, infant mortality declined, and he attributes this to the adoption of breast-feeding where formerly it had not been practised or at best practised for a short period. He also quotes D. Glass on the subject: O. Turpeinen, 'Fertility and Mortality in England since 1750', *Population Studies*, 33 (1979), no. 1. See also C. Rollet, 'Allaitement, mise en nourrice et mortalité infantile en France à la fin du XIX', *Population*, 33 (1978), no. 6, who attributes the lower infant mortality of the South to the longer duration of the breast-feeding period.

53 J.-L. Muret was among the first to discuss the matter in the light of comparative data. In Holland, out of 1,000 deaths in the first year, 890 occurred in the first six months after birth; the corresponding figure in Vevey is 819, in Pays de Vaud 730 and in Berlin 749: J.-L. Muret, *Mémoire sur l'état de la population dans le pays de Vaud* (Yverdon, 1766), part II, pp. 108–9. In France, according to a sample published by INED, during the period 1740–89, 823 deaths out of 1,000 happened in the first six months after birth.

54 M. Breschi and M. Livi-Bacci, 'Saison et climat comme contraintes de la survie des enfants. L'expérience italienne au XIXème siècle', *Population*, 41 (1986), no. 1, pp. 9–36. Infant mortality in the Veneto was about twice as high for babies born in winter as for those born in summer; in other areas of northern Italy the variation was less extreme. In more northern countries with colder climates, such as Belgium, Germany and France, little or no variation was observed between winter and summer births.

55 Turpeinen in 'Infectious Diseases' attributes high infant mortality among populations of the western coast of West Bothnia to the recurrent absences of seafaring fathers, which threw the weight of agricultural work on women and caused in turn their absence from the home.

56 This probably explains the extremely high infant mortality differential between the social classes in Geneva. See Perrenoud, 'L'inégalité sociale devant la mort'.

5 Food and standard of living: hypotheses and controversies

1 Less recent general works on this topic are J. C. Drummond and A. Wilbraham, *The Englishman's Food. A History of Five Centuries of English Diet* (London, 1939), second edn. by D. Hollingsworth (London, 1957); A. Maurizio, *Histoire de l'alimentation végétale* (Paris, 1932). Among more recent studies to which I draw attention are those in *Annales ESC*, particularly J.-J. Hémardinquer (ed.), *Pour une histoire de l'alimentation*, *Cahier des Annales*, no. 28 (Paris, 1970), and the volume devoted to the *Histoire de la consommation*, *Annales ESC*, 30 (1975), nos. 2–3, pp. 402–632. Also useful in this context is H. Neveux's article, 'L'alimentation du XIVe au XVIIIe siècle', *Revue d'Histoire Économique et Sociale*, 51 (1973), no. 3, pp. 336–79; also F. Braudel's vast work, *Civilization matérielle, économie et capitalisme, XVe–XVIIIe siècles*, vol. I: *Les structures du quotidien: le possible et l'impossible*, pp. 81–228. For Italy, see M. S. Mazzi, 'Note per una storia dell'alimentazione medievale', *Studi di storia medievale e moderna in onore di Ernesto Sestan* (Florence, 1980), vol. I, pp. 57–102.

2 A. E. and D. A. Bender, *Nutrition for Medical Students* (London, Wiley, 1982).

3 It is often pointed out in studies on nutrition that these 'average' estimates

of consumption or nutritional requirement are less significant the larger the population sampled. It is not, however, the size of the population but the variations it conceals that make such estimates difficult to use. Rural populations, for instance, were presumably much more homogeneous from the point of view of what they ate than urban ones, and were at the same time much more numerous.

4 Neveux, 'L'alimentation', p. 372.
5 D. Zanetti, *Problemi alimentari di un'economia pre-industriale* (Turin, Boringhieri, 1965), pp. 60–1.
6 Neveux, 'L'alimentation', p. 378.
7 M. Morineau, 'Post-scriptum. De la Hollande à la France' in Hémardinquer (ed.), *Pour une histoire de l'alimentation*, pp. 115–25.
8 J.-C. Toutain, 'La consommation alimentaire en France de 1789 à 1964', *Economie et Société*, Cahier de l'ISEA, vol. A, no. 11 (Geneva, 1971), pp. 1919–20. The correction is implicit if one uses the 'high' estimate for bread consumption, rather than the 'low' one used by Toutain for his calculation of caloric intake.
9 M. Morineau, 'Révolution agricole, révolution alimentaire, révolution démographique', *Annales de Démographie Historique*, 1974, pp. 340–1.
10 E. F. Heckscher, *An Economic History of Sweden* (Cambridge, Mass., Harvard University Press, 1954), pp. 69, 116 and 149; W. Abel, *Congiuntura agraria e crisi agrarie* (Turin, Einaudi, 1976), pp. 234–5, 295.
11 Abel, *Congiuntura agraria*, p. 211.
12 S. Somogyi, 'L'alimentazione dell'Italia' in *Storia d'Italia* (Turin, Einaudi, 1973), vol. V, p. 893.
13 Toutain, 'La consommation alimentaire en France', pp. 1994–5.
14 My calculations based on ISTAT estimates, *Statistiche storiche dell'Italia 1861–1975* (Rome, 1976), p. 159.
15 L. Gallo, *Alimentazione e demografia nella Grecia antica* (Salerno, Laveglia, 1984), p. 31.
16 Somogyi, 'L'alimentazione dell'Italia', p. 842.
17 Estimates of caloric intake can differ according to the stage of processing at which one takes the raw materials. For instance, 100 g of wheat contain roughly 320 calories, 100 g of white flour roughly 340 and 100 g of bread around 250 calories. On the other hand, 1 kg. of wheat will produce a lesser quantity of flour (depending on how finely it is milled), although this amount of flour will in turn produce a weight of bread equal to, or greater than, that of the grain from which it came. However, we shall pursue this discussion about relative weights and their caloric equivalents no further, since they are largely dependent on local techniques and blends of flour.
18 M. Aymard, 'Pour l'histoire de l'alimentation. Quelques remarques de méthode', *Annales ESC*, 30 (1975), nos. 2–3, p. 432.
19 F. Galiani, *Della moneta* (Milan, Feltrinelli, 1970), p. 54.
20 Abel, *Congiuntura agraria*, pp. 104–7 and 382–3.
21 Abel, *Congiuntura agraria*, pp. 105–6. See also I. Blanchard, 'The Continental European Cattle Trade, 1400–1600', *Economic History Review*, 2nd series, 39 (1986), no. 3, p. 453.
22 Neveux, 'L'alimentation', p. 370. See also C. Dyer, 'Changes in Nutrition and Standard of Living in England, 1200–1500', *Ninth Economic History Congress* (Bern, 1986). Sir John Fortescue's dictum in *De Landibus Legum*

Angliae (London, 1600), chapter 36, is quoted in E. P. Prentice, *Hunger and History* (New York, Harper and Brothers, 1939), p. 61. The same opinion is expressed in Drummond and Wilbraham, *The Englishman's Food*, p. 49: 'There is little doubt that large quantities of beef, mutton and veal were being eaten at this time.'

23 A. M. Nada Patrone, *Il cibo del ricco ed il cibo del povero. Contributo alla storia qualitativa dell'alimentazione. L'area pedemontana negli ultimi secoli del medioevo* (Turin, Centro Studi Piemontesi, 1981), pp. 221–3.

24 A. Giuffrida, 'Considerazioni sul consumo di carne a Palermo nei secoli XIV e XV', *Mélanges de l'Ecole Française à Rome*, 87 (1975), no. 2, pp. 583–95.

25 M. S. Mazzi, 'Note per la storia dell'alimentazione', p. 88. See also M. Montanari, *L'alimentazione contadina nell'alto Medioevo* (Naples, Liguori, 1979); Idem, *Alimentazione e cultura nel Medioevo* (Roma-Bari, Laterza, 1988).

26 B. Bennassar and J. Goy, 'Contribution à l'histoire de la consommation du XIVème au XIXème siècle', *Annales ESC*, 30 (1975), nos. 2–3, p. 427. For Eastern Europe, see also A. Wyczanski and M. Dembínska, 'La nourriture en Europe Centrale au début de l'Age Moderne', *Ninth Economic History Congress* (Bern, 1986). According to Drummond and Wilbraham, *The Englishman's Food*, p. 47, 'in the good years they [the peasants] were well nourished, probably considerably better than the poor country people in the rest of Europe'.

27 Braudel, *Les structures du quotidien*, p. 162.

28 See Blanchard, 'The European Cattle Trade'.

29 Neveux, 'L'alimentation', p. 363.

30 Neveux, 'L'alimentation', p. 363.

31 Abel, *Congiuntura agraria*, p. 383. See also Drummond and Wilbraham, *The Englishman's Food*, p. 99.

32 Toutain, 'La consommation alimentaire en France', p. 1947.

33 ISTAT, *Statistiche storiche*, p. 159.

34 J. W. Goethe, *Italienische Reise (1786–1788)*.

35 There is a large literature on this topic. I refer the reader to Braudel's summaries, *Les structures du quotidien*, pp. 136–43, and B. H. Slicher Van Bath, *Storia agraria dell'Europa Occidentale (1500–1850)* (Turin, Einaudi, 1972), pp. 363–88. As for potatoes, see R. N. Salaman, *The History and Social Influence of the Potato* (Cambridge, Cambridge University Press, 1949).

36 For an up-to-date version of this classic opinion see M. W. Flinn, 'The Stabilization of Mortality in Pre-Industrial Europe', *Journal of European Economic History*, 3 (1974), no. 2, pp. 309–11.

37 Slicher Van Bath, *Storia agraria*, p. 128.

38 Quoted by K. H. Connell, *The Population of Ireland* (Oxford, Clarendon Press, 1950), p. 122.

39 Slicher Van Bath, *Storia agraria*, p. 368, maintains that the productivity of maize could be double or triple that of wheat. P. M. Hohenberg, 'Maize in French Agriculture', *The Journal of European Economic History*, 6 (1977), no. 1, pp. 73–9, puts it for south-west France at only one and a half times that of wheat.

40 Slicher Van Bath, *Storia agraria*, p. 367.

41 Abel, *Congiuntura agraria*, pp. 308–9. See also G. B. Masefield, 'Crops and

Livestock', in E. E. Rich and C. Wilson (eds.), *The Economy of Expanding Europe in the Sixteenth and Seventeenth Centuries, The Cambridge Economic History of Europe*, vol. IV (Cambridge, Cambridge University Press, 1967), pp. 344–7.

42 L. Messedaglia, *Il mais e la vita rurale in Italia* (Piacenza, Federazione Italiana dei Consorzi Agrari, 1927), and by the same author, *Per la storia dell'agricoltura e dell'alimentazione* (Piacenza, Federazione Italiana dei Consorzi Agrari, 1932). Also Ministero di Agricoltura, Industria e Commercio, 'La pellagra in Italia', *Annali di Agricoltura*, 18 (1979), Appendix.

43 M. Livi-Bacci, 'Fertility, Nutrition and Pellagra: Italy during the Vital Revolution', *Journal of Interdisciplinary History*, 16 (1986), no. 3, p. 443.

44 W. L. Langer, 'American Foods and Europe's Population Growth, 1750–1850', *Journal of Social History*, 1 (1975), pp. 51–61.

45 Connell, *The Population of Ireland*, p. 160.

46 W. Cobbett, 'Letters of William Cobbett to Charles Marshall', in G. D. H. and M. Cole (eds.), *Rural Rides*, vol. III (London, Peter Davies, 1930), pp. 899–900.

47 Salaman, *The History and Social Influence of the Potato*, pp. 613–17; and P. E. Razzell, 'An Interpretation of the Modern Rise of Population in Europe – a Critique', *Population Studies*, 28 (1974), no. 1, p. 8.

48 C. Vanderbroeke, 'Cultivation and Consumption of the Potato in the Seventeenth and Eighteenth Centuries', *Acta Historiae Neerlandicae*, 5 (1971), p. 35. See also M. Morineau, *Pour une histoire économique vraie* (Lille, Presses Universitaires de Lille, 1985), pp. 121–39. F. Mendels, *Industrialisation and Population Pressure in Eighteenth-Century Flanders* (New York, Arno Press, 1981), pp. 132–3.

49 Livi-Bacci, 'Fertility', pp. 441–2.

50 Hohenberg, 'Maize', pp. 70 and 72.

51 R. N. Salaman, *The Influence of the Potato in the Course of Irish History* (Dublin, Browne and Nolan, 1943), p. 30.

52 'The influence of food on the population size in history was basically determined by the relationship between nutrition level and response to infectious disease', T. McKeown states in 'Food, Infection and Population', *Journal of Interdisciplinary History*, 14 (1983), no. 2, p. 29.

53 Morineau, 'Révolution agricole', pp. 348–54.

54 This is Connell's opinion in *The Population of Ireland*. He maintains that the success of the potato as a staple, and the consequent rise in agricultural productivity, stimulated the fragmentation of land and the formation of new households where previously people had been forced to wait for the tenant's death before a piece of land became available.

55 F. Braudel, *Civilization matérielle, économie et capitalisme, vol. III: Les temps du monde* (Paris, Colin, 1979), p. 532.

56 B. Thomas, 'Food Supply in the United Kingdom during the Industrial Revolution', in J. Mokyr (ed.), *The Economics of the Industrial Revolution* (Totowa, New Jersey, Rowman and Allanheld, 1985), pp. 140–2. See also E. L. Jones, 'Agriculture, 1700–1800', in R. Floud and D. McCloskey (eds.), *The Economic History of Britain since 1700*, vol. I (Cambridge, Cambridge University Press, 1981).

57 C. H. Feinstein, 'Capital Accumulation and the Industrial Revolution', in Floud and Closkey (eds.), *The Economic History*, pp. 135–7. According to

Feinstein, real consumption per head varied between £9.6 and £10.5 per
annum between 1760 and 1810, reached £11.3 between 1811 and 1820, and
started thereafter a long increasing trend (£14.6 1821–30).

58 Drummond and Wilbraham, *The Englishman's Food*, pp. 171–3 and 206;
and Razzell, 'An Interpretation', pp. 8–9.

59 B. Thomas, 'Food Supply', p. 144.

60 *Ibid.*, p. 149.

61 G. Fridlizius, 'The Mortality Decline in the First Phase of the Demographic
Transition: Swedish Experiences', in T. Bengtsson, G. Fridlizius and R.
Ohlsson (eds.), *Pre-Industrial Population Change* (Stockholm, Almquist and
Wiksell, 1984), p. 82.

62 Fridlizius, 'The Mortality Decline', p. 81.

63 G. Prato, *La vita economica in Piemonte a mezzo il secolo XVIII* (Turin, 1908),
pp. 462–3.

64 S. Pugliese, *Due secoli di vita agricola* (Turin, Bocca, 1908).

65 V. Perez Moreda, *Las crisis de mortalidad en la España interior, siglos XVI–XIX*
(Madrid, Siglo Veinteuno, 1980), p. 408.

66 Braudel, *Les structures du quotidien*, p. 171.

67 Abel, *Congiuntura agraria*, p. 383.

68 For construction workers in Florence, see R. A. Goldthwaite, *The Building
of Renaissance Florence* (Baltimore, The John Hopkins University Press,
1980), pp. 287–350.

69 Abel, *Congiuntura agraria*, p. 383.

70 Toutain, 'La consommation alimentaire en France', p. 1911.

71 Montanari, *L'alimentazione contadina*, p. 309.

72 B. Kerblay, 'L'évolution de l'alimentation rurale en Russie 1896–1960',
Pour une histoire de l'alimentation, J. J. Hémardinquer (ed.), *Cahiers des
Annales*, 28 (1970), 46, p. 901.

73 Quoted by Abel, *Congiuntura agraria*, p. 235.

74 *Ibid.*, p. 236.

75 For a less pessimistic view of the course of workers' real wages between
1765 and 1820, see P. H. Lindert and J. G. Williamson, 'English Workers'
Living Standards during the Industrial Revolution: A New Look', *Economic History Review*, 2nd series, 36 (1983), no. 1.

76 There seems to be a consensus of opinion among researchers that
mortality crises in most of Europe had lost virulence by the eighteenth
century. However, see Flinn, 'The Stabilization of Mortality', and L. Del
Panta, *Le epidemie nella storia demografica italiana (secoli XIV–XIX)* (Turin,
Loescher, 1980).

77 By 'years of severe mortality crisis' we mean those years where the number of deaths was three times that calculated as normal for the period. See
Del Panta, *Le epidemie*, p. 132. My estimates for 1550–99 are based on data
taken from L. Del Panta, 'Cronologia e diffusione delle crisi di mortalità in
Toscana dalla fine del XIV secolo agli inizi del XIX secolo', *Ricerche Storiche*,
7 (1977), no. 2. The real-wages series come from Goldthwaite, *The Building*, pp. 438–9.

78 Braudel, *Les structures du quotidien*, p. 109.

79 Y. Blayo, 'La mortalité en France 1740 à 1829', *Population*, special no.
(November 1975), pp. 123–42.

80 Since one day's work could buy you 0.2 staio (1 staio=18 kg.; 0.2

staio=3.6 kg.), it took 27.8 days of work, equivalent to nearly 300 hours of work, to buy a quintal (100 kg.). In the fifteenth century, real wages rose often to a staio or more a day, enabling the purchase of 100 kg. of wheat over 5.6 days of work, equivalent to 50 to 60 working hours.

81 Direzione Generale di Statistica, *Risultati dell'inchiesta sulle condizioni igieniche e sanitarie nei comuni del Regno, Relazione Generale* (Rome, Tipografia in San Michele, 1886), p. 142.

82 So maintains V. Perez Moreda, 'Hambre, mortalidad y crecimiento en las poblaciones de la Europa preindustrial', *Revista de Historia Economica*, 6 (1988), no. 3.

83 R. W. Fogel *et al.*, 'Secular Changes in American and British Stature and Nutrition', in R. I. Rotberg and T. K. Rabb (eds.), *Hunger and History* (Cambridge, Cambridge University Press, 1985), pp. 247–83.

84 P. B. Eveleth and J. M. Tanner, *Worldwide Variations in Human Growth* (Cambridge, Cambridge University Press, 1976); J. M. Tanner, *A History of the Study of Human Growth* (Cambridge, Cambridge University Press, 1981).

85 For the factors of growth, see Tanner's classic, *A History*.

86 This aspect is played down by Fogel in 'Secular Changes', pp. 253 and ff.

87 J. Komlos, 'Patterns of Children's Growth in the Habsburg Monarchy: the Standards of Living and Economic Development in the Eighteenth Century', *The American Historical Review*, 90 (1985), no. 5.

88 Fogel, 'Secular Changes', p. 265.

89 *Ibid.*, p. 266.

90 L. G. Sandberg and R. Steckel, 'Soldier, Soldier, What Made you Grow so Tall?', *Economy and History*, 23 (1980), no. 2, pp. 91–105.

91 R. Floud and K. Wachter, 'Poverty and Physical Stature', *Social Science History*, 6 (1982), no. 4, pp. 432–3.

92 J. Komlos, 'Patterns of Children's Growth in East-Central Europe in the Eighteenth Century', *Annals of Human Biology*, 13 (1986), no. 1, pp. 33–48.

93 H. Wurm, 'Über die Schwankungender Durchschnittlichen Körperhöhe', *Homo*, 33 (1982), no. 1, p. 297.

94 Tanner, *A History*, p. 297.

6 Antagonism and adaptation

1 E. N. Wilmsen, 'Studies in Diet, Nutrition and Fertility among a Group of Kalahari Bushmen in Botswana', *Social Science Information*, 21 (1982) no. 1, p. 102. V. Valverde, H. Delgado, R. Martorell, J. M. Delizan, V. Mejia-Pivaral and R. E. Klein, *Seasonality and Nutritional Status*, INCAP, publ. I-1249 (Guatemala, 1982).

2 World Health Organization, *Energy and Proteins Requirements. Report of a joint FAO/WHO/UN Expert Consultation* (Technical Reports Series no. 729, Geneva, 1985), pp. 28–9. The research shows that boys whose growth is 'stunted' have better cardio-respiratory, muscular and general physical efficiency than their normal peers. Contrary to expectation, retarded growth does not seem to have an overall detrimental effect later in adult life, at least for activities which do not require particular physical strength.

3 A. Ferro Luzzi, 'Range of Variation in Energy Expenditure and Scope for Regulation' in *Proceedings of the XIII International Congress of Nutrition*

(Brighton, 1985), pp. 397–8. See also W. A. Stini, 'Adaptive Strategies of Human Populations under Nutritional Stress' in E. S. Watts, F. S. Johnston and G. W. Lasker (eds.), *Biosocial Interrelations in Population Adaptation* (The Hague, Mouton, 1975), pp. 19–41. Also by the same author, 'Body Composition and Nutrient Reserves' in D. N. Walcher and N. Kretchmer (eds.), *Evolutionary Perspective*, 1980, pp. 107–20.

4 A. Frisancho, T. Velasquez and J. Sanchez, 'Possible Adaptive Significance of Small Body Size in the Attainment of Aerobic Capacity Among High-Altitude Quechua Natives', *Biosocial Interrelations*, pp. 55–64. See also the series of studies on the biology of Andean populations in P. T. Baker and M. A. Little (eds.), *Man in the Andes* (Stroudsburg, Pennsylvania, Dowden Hutchinson and Ross, 1976).

5 Stini, 'Body Composition', p. 113.

6 G. Lasker and M. Womack, 'An Anatomical View of Demographic Data: Biomass, Fat Mass and Lean Body Mass of the United States and Mexican Human Population', *Biosocial Interrelations*, p. 50.

7 On the subject of the relationship between nutritional stress and adaptability, see P. T. Baker, 'The Adaptive Limits of Human Populations', *Man*, 19 (1983), pp. 1–14; M. T. Newman, 'Ecology and Nutritional Stress in Man', *American Anthropologist*, 64 (1962), pp. 22–34.

8 A. Ivanovsky, 'Physical Modifications of the Population in Russia under Famine', *American Journal of Physical Anthropology*, 6 (1923), no. 4, pp. 331–53. See also World Health Organization, *Energy*, p. 21.

9 R. Martorell, 'Genetics, Environment and Growth: Issues in the Assessment of Nutritional Status' in A. Velasquez and H. Bourges (eds.), *Genetic Factors in Nutrition* (New York, Academic Press, 1984), pp. 373–4. See also WHO, *Energy*, p. 21.

10 E. S. Wing and A. B. Brown, *Paleonutrition* (New York, Academic Press, 1979), pp. 173–4.

11 R. L. Wirsing, 'The Health of Traditional Societies and the Effects of Acculturation', *Current Anthropology*, 26 (1985), no. 3, pp. 303–22.

12 Just as the sudden change in traditional methods in upbringing and nutrition in very early childhood is at the root of the continued high mortality of so many countries in equatorial Africa.

13 See also note 59 of chapter three.

14 If we assume that the death-rate and the birth-rate are both at 40 per thousand, one can imagine that famine could raise the former by 75 per cent and lower the latter by 25 per cent, which corresponds to values of 70 and 30 per thousand respectively, with a rate of growth therefore equal to −40 per thousand.

15 This is approximately equal to the European average for the eighteenth century.

16 If we assume a normal rate of growth of 2 per thousand, after a century the population free from crises would have grown by 22.1 per cent and one with crises by 3.6 per cent. If, on the other hand, we assume a normal rate of growth of 6 per thousand, then the increases would be respectively 81.9 and 42.7 per cent. See also S. C. Watkins and J. Menken, 'Famines in Historical Perspective', *Population and Development Review*, 11 (1985), no. 5, pp. 647–75. The authors use a complex method of simulation to calculate the effect of varying degrees of famine on the size of a population, the

time taken to return to levels prior to the crisis, and so on. They reached the curious conclusion that famines were not common enough to act as an effective check on demographic growth (p. 665) and they extend this conclusion to all mortality crises (p. 666). This is odd when one considers the effects of the plague cycles or the mere fact that – if one goes by the authors' example in the present text which, interestingly enough, agrees with the results of Watkins and Menken – the elimination of crises would have doubled the rate of growth.

17 T. K. Helleiner, 'The Population of Europe from the Black Death to the Eve of the Vital Revolution' in *The Economy of Expanding Europe in the Sixteenth and Seventeenth Centuries*, E. E. Rich and C. Wilson (eds.), *The Cambridge Economic History of Europe* (Cambridge, Cambridge University Press, 1967), vol. IV. It is worth recalling Albert Camus' apt phrase, which Helleiner quotes at the close of his essay, 'personne ne sera jamais libre tant qu'il y aura des fléaux' [no-one will ever be free as long as there are plagues].

18 J. D. Chambers, *Population, Economy and Society in Pre-Industrial England* (London, Oxford University Press, 1972), p. 87.

19 This area is dealt with excellently by R. M. Anderson and R. M. May in 'Population Biology and Infectious Diseases', *Nature*, 280 (1979), 2 and 8 August.

20 These considerations are very simplified and only apply to an exclusively rural population with stagnant productivity. The growth of towns, the development of the service industries, proto-industrialisation and the birth of the manufacturing industries introduce a more complex set of variables into the discussion and land loses the restrictive role it occupied in demographic growth.

21 C. T. Smith, *An Historical Geography of Western Europe before 1800* (London, Longmans, Green and Co. Ltd., 1967), chapter 5.

22 Smith, *Geografia*, p. 601.

23 W. Abel, *Congiuntura agraria e crisi agrarie* (Turin, Einaudi, 1976), p. 308.

24 B. H. Slicher Van Bath, *Storia agraria dell'Europa Occidentale (1500–1850)* (Turin, Einaudi, 1972).

25 T. Mann, *La filosofia di Nietzsche* (Milan, Mondadori, 1980), p. 89.

Index

Abel, W., 92, 93, 101–2
Adaptation, of the energy requirements in case of famine, 42, 47, 61; metabolism of the mother, 75; to the constraint factors, 111–12; in the short term, 111–12; in the medium and long term, 111–12
Aja, 45
Alps, populations with deficiency-related diseases, 30
America, life expectancy, 68; average height of the army recruits, 109
Amsterdam, 45
Anghiari, 60
Animals, growth strategies, 8
Antagonism, between malnutrition and infection, 38; between resources and survival, 111
Antwerp, food budgets, 87
Arezzo, 60
Argentina, life expectancy, 68; meat consumption, 68
Arles, caloric budget of the Bishop's table, 63–4
Augustus, population in his times, 1
Austria, average height of the army recruits, 109

Balkans, foodstuffs availability, 99
Banbury, infant mortality, 74
Bangladesh, relationship between malnutrition and immunity, 36; famine, 44
Basic metabolism, 42; its reduction in case of nutritional stress, 42, 112
Bassin Parisien, 15
Beauvais, prices, 55
Beer, consumption, 116
Belgium, infant mortality, 74

Benedict, XIV, 41
Bergemoletto, 41
Body growth, and nutritional stress, 112
Body weight and caloric requirements, 23; reduction in case of half-fasting, 42; reduction in case of famine, 45, 47
Bologna, famine of 1602, 49
Bosnia, average height of the army recruits, 109
Brazil, life expectancy, 68
Bread, caloric yield and price, 85; predominance in the diet, 87–91
Breast-feeding, 10, 75–6; its immunological value, 76
Budget, food budget or caloric one, xiii; in France, Japan and Italy, 30–1; difficulties for the valuation, 80; soldiers and sailors from several countries, 81
Buenos Aires, life expectancy, 68
Bushmen, seasonal caloric budget, 112

Caltanissetta, 93
Canada, typhus, 49; life expectancy, 68
Canalis, 35
Carbohydrates, 27
Carpathians, populations with deficiency-related diseases, 30
Celibacy, in Ireland, 16
Cereals, prices and famine, 48, 54, 55, 56; home consumption, 48; international trade, 48; their prevalence in the diet, 48, 85, 87–91; cost in terms of hours of work, 106
Checks, preventive checks and repressive ones according to Malthus, 11–13; repressive checks and their role in the short and long term, 119
Childe, V. G., 20

145

Cambridge Studies in Population, Economy and Society in Past Time

Titles available in paperback are marked with an asterisk.